the
balanced
innovator

the
balanced
innovator

turning ideas
into reality

robert carter

The Balanced Innovator: Turning Ideas into Reality

Copyright © 2008 Robert Carter. All rights reserved. No part of this book may be reproduced or retransmitted in any form or by any means without the written permission of the publisher.

Published by Wheatmark™
610 East Delano Street, Suite 104
Tucson, Arizona 85705 U.S.A.
www.wheatmark.com

International Standard Book Number: 978-1-58736-950-6
Library of Congress Control Number: 2007939075

contents

Preface vii
Acknowledgment and Thanks xiii
Introduction xv

Chapter 1	What Is Innovation?	1
Chapter 2	Some Background on Six Sigma	10
Chapter 3	Innovation and Six Sigma	18
Chapter 4	Six Sigma in a Smaller Business	29
Chapter 5	5-D Project Success	37
Chapter 6	Why World-Class Is Not Enough	45
Chapter 7	Unparalyze the Paradigm	51
Chapter 8	What Is Growth, Anyway?	58
Chapter 9	The Chorus of the Customer	75
Chapter 10	The Chorus Is Everywhere and Always	82
Chapter 11	Business Development Is an Activity, Not Just a Department's Name	89
Chapter 12	Love the Customer	96
Chapter 13	Irrelevantize the Competition	99
Chapter 14	Hurdle the Barrier	104
Chapter 15	Developing Your What, How, Why Balance	112
Chapter 16	Some Thoughts on Leadership	115
Chapter 17	3-2-1 Blastoff	122
Chapter 18	Conclusion	131
Chapter 19	Recommended Further Reading	134
Appendix A	Brief Description of Some Tools and Methods . .	141
Appendix B	Bibliography	149

preface

At age twenty-three, Winston Churchill wrote in an unpublished paper on oratory, *The Scaffolding of Rhetoric,*[1] "Before you can inspire with emotion, you must be swamped with it yourself. Before you can move their tears, your own must flow. To convince them, you must yourself believe." I believe in the principles and ideas in *The Balanced Innovator*. I have tried them and seen them work. I have seen time and again that success depends on the balance between our intellectual, organizational, and human factors—in other words, a balance between what we do, know, and understand; how we do things and learn; and especially in why we do things. This balance between the What, How, and Why is the key to success in life and especially in Innovation. Why we do something validates What we do and How we do it, and vice versa.

Success is also dependent on strong, positive emotional connections, and those are driven by purpose and passion. Without purpose, we don't know why our actions are important; if we don't understand why things are important, we have little or no passion for them. All the skills, knowledge, and experience in the world (the What factors) mean little if we have no emotional connection, passion, or purpose (the Why factors). Likewise, passion and purpose with low skills, knowledge, and experience is equally doomed to failure. How we organize ourselves to complete our actions and develop our skills is the third key factor. To achieve success, we need to balance the What of our intellectual strengths with the How of our organizational skills

---

1   Montablo, Thomas, *Seven Lessons in Speechmaking from one of the Greatest Orators of All Time*, 1969, The Churchill Centre.

and the Why of our human factors. I call this the *What, How, Why Balance,* and I've used it as the basis for many of the themes in *The Balanced Innovator.*

The greatest and most successful people in history had this balance; they knew what to do, how to do it, and why they were doing it. In other words, they had knowledge, skills, and a purpose.

Author and pastor Rick Warren is balanced. As of September 2007, his book *The Purpose-Driven Life* has spent 236 weeks on the *USA Today* best-seller list and is one of the most popular nonfiction books in history, selling more than 25 million copies. Why? It appeals to people all over the world by helping them achieve a purpose, which is done in part because of the balance between their intellectual, organizational, and human (and in this case, spiritual) factors. Former British prime minister Margaret Thatcher was balanced, and so was the first president of the United States, George Washington. Industrialists Henry Ford and John D. Rockefeller, and inventor Thomas Edison, were also balanced. So, too, are TV personality Oprah Winfrey, movie director Stephen Spielberg, and composer Andrew Lloyd Webber.

American industrialist Andrew Carnegie was at one time the richest man in the world. He knew what to do and how to do it, and he knew why it was important for him to succeed. He spent the first half of his life amassing a vast fortune and the second half giving it all away again; both actions were always part of his plan. He had the intellectual, organizational, and human skills, and he was emotionally connected to his vision. Carnegie lived his life in the What, How, Why Balance.

Swedish inventor and industrialist Alfred Nobel ended his life well balanced. A great scientist, he was in danger of being known for his use of nitroglycerine in explosive weapons. During one disastrous experiment, his younger brother Emil and several coworkers were killed. Alfred Nobel redirected his life and became a pioneer for both peace and literature, and his legacy lives in the awards that bear his name.

In wartime, Winston Churchill had this balance; he was one of the greatest leaders of the twentieth century. His strong purpose was supported by a tremendous intellect and fine organizational skills.

Strangely, once the war was over and victory was secured, he lost his purpose; in other words, he no longer had balance. He lost the next general election in Great Britain and was never again elected to be prime minister.

Success throughout history shows dependence on this balance. Peacemaker and moral leader of India Mahatma Gandhi was balanced; he knew the what, how, and why. Through his moral authority, he united the people of India and brought the British Empire to its knees—an amazing achievement for a man who was never elected to office.

I encourage you to think for a moment about the successful people in your life. If I were a betting man, I would wager that almost without exception, lasting success is due to a balance between the intellectual, organizational, and human factors in a person's life—the What, How, Why Balance.

One of the greatest sporting coaches in history is Sir Alex Ferguson, the manager of England's Manchester United Football Club. When he took the reins in 1987, the team was in a state of turmoil. They were perennial underachievers who hadn't been champions of England for more than twenty years. A further twenty years down the road, and Manchester United has won nine Premiership titles, plus countless other trophies. The current team has the potential to become the most exciting in history. Fergie (as he is known by fans) has always maintained balance between the three factors, even when United was in the doldrums for a couple of seasons as he rebuilt the team. Furthermore, Manchester United is the biggest sports organization in the world, with a net worth of over $2 billion and more than 75 million fans across the globe.

It is my strong belief that people who have the What, How, Why Balance between their intellectual, organizational, and human factors are more successful than people who don't. Organizations that have this balance are more successful than those that don't.

Successful Innovation is a prime example of dependence on this balance. The greatest invention or idea in the world will be a commercial flop if it is difficult to acquire (lack of organizational factors) or if there is no emotional connection with potential customers (lack of human factors).

Strong, positive emotional connections can be so powerful that they inspire. Falling in love is one of these powerful emotions; similarly, our memories are based on those emotions. Whether the need is personal or organizational, success is heavily dependent on emotion. Successful Innovation is no different.

We always prefer to do business with people we like and trust, people we have strong emotional connections with. We marry because of the strong, positive emotional connection we make with our spouse. We often make major decisions emotionally and then try to justify them with logic. Underestimate the power of emotion at your peril.

My desire is to develop a strong emotional connection with you—the reader of this book—by sharing my knowledge and experience. More importantly, I hope you will make stronger, more positive emotional connections with everybody you know. My vision is to generate benefit to society and the economy, through the creation of a significant number of noble jobs. You can help me to achieve this vision by enabling the organizations you belong to and the companies you work for to achieve the What, How, Why Balance. They will in turn become more successful.

A key ingredient to a thriving society and economy is successful Innovation. *The Balanced Innovator* provides a framework for success by combining proven experience with the best contemporary strategic thinking of our time. Although the focus is Innovation, the ideas in this book are not limited to business. They apply to everything that you do: socially, spiritually, vocationally, and even in your relationships. Leaders, managers, employees, professors, students, pastors, husbands, wives, and children of all ages can benefit. If everything we do is focused on making society a better place to live, we all benefit.

I believe that all people are responsible for their personal growth and the growth of the organizations they work for or belong to. I believe that we must truly love the people we know, including our customers and coworkers, and that our behaviors must prove this love. We can achieve this through the What, How, Why Balance of our intellectual, organizational, and human factors.

Believe in yourself and trust in others. Help your family, friends, and colleagues to believe, and together we can make this world a better place.

Robert Carter
In2theStratosphere@msn.com

acknowledgment and thanks

There are way too many folks to thank, but here are a few key ones: Jim and Eileen, my parents; James Jen, Charlie, Joe, and Lexi, my kids; Teresa, my loving and very patient wife; and my sister Andrea and her husband Phil (sorry about City).

On a professional note: Jim Rayburn, Jon Mckenzie, Bernie Saboe, Rusty Patterson, Stuart Edamura, Linda May, Robin Lawton, Ron Morgan, Ed Cobleigh, Steve McElroy, Ralph Stacey, Harry Davis, Alan Garwood, Rob Ryder, Keith Richardson, Steve Shelton, Julie Nitzschke, Bob Anstee, Steve Sanders, Ian Frain, Ron Shields, Jeff Poole, John Onion, and Dr. George Connor. All have positively affected my life. There are dozens of others, too.

I shall not mention those who have negatively affected my life, even though they probably are expecting to see their names in print. You know who you are and I forgive you, mainly because I have become stronger thanks to your influence.

Finally, I'd also like to thank anybody else I have met or am about to meet, authors of books I've forgotten to mention and those who I haven't yet heard of, and those business leaders who are going to benefit as well as those who don't need any help because their buggy whip is better than anybody else's.

introduction

The primary focus of this book is Innovation and in particular, how Innovation leads to business growth. In order to understand the relationship between Innovation and growth, it is necessary to first understand why some new product development (NPD) projects are successful while others fail. Funding the right NPD projects is a key leadership challenge that can make or break an organization. I have found that in almost every case, successful NPD projects are balanced. This is also true in the area of new business proposals, another subject that I have studied extensively over the last few years. Like NPD projects, winning proposals have a balanced approach to the solution. Innovation is the key ingredient in both NPD projects and new business proposals, so the key to successful Innovation is balance. Balanced Innovation is where the intellectual, human, and organizational factors validate each other. The intellectual factors are What you know, do, and are (like science, technology, and engineering); the organizational factors are How you learn, How you solve issues, and How you plan and organize; the human factors are the emotional connections you make, the behaviors you exhibit, the way you tell your story, and Why you do what you do. So success is dependent on the What, How, Why Balance.

Organizations should focus their investment funding on balanced projects. This doesn't mean that unbalanced projects aren't worth considering, but the project leader should have a plan of action to achieve balance as part of the development program. *The Balanced Innovator* addresses those needs and helps you achieve the What, How, Why Balance.

The Creative Age

One of my goals is to stretch you to think about new ways to enable success in this shrinking world of outsourcing and automation. The Industrial Age is long gone, as is the Information Age of the knowledge worker. We are now in a mix of the Conceptual Age,[1] where design and beauty are far more important than mere functionality, and the Entertainment Age,[2] where everything we do seems to revolve around having fun. This new age is often called the *Creative Age*.[3]

The management techniques and methods we used in the Industrial and Information Ages may not be relevant today, yet we still use them in abundance. One of these methods may be the exception: Six Sigma has been incredibly successful as an analytical tool to help reduce variation and improve quality. The Six Sigma methodology can also be a key enabler as we embrace the Creative Age. Because I have found it to be a powerful enabler for Innovation, you will find many references to Six Sigma in this book. However, the ideas and principles you will read about can also be applied without Six Sigma (or other improvement method), should you desire.

Many thought leaders, such as authors and Innovation consultants like Daniel Pink, Gene D Cohen, and Robert Rosenfeld[4], believe that success in these changing times will rely much more on right-brain thinking. Pink tells us in *A Whole New Mind* of many scientific studies to support these claims, such as the study of brains under various levels of stress being undertaken at the National Institute of Mental Health near Washington, D.C. There are many new techniques being used as well, such as fMRI (functional Magnetic Resonance Imaging) and creative thinking pioneer and author Ned Herrmann's brain dominance model.[5] After more than twenty years working in the business world, I can see that Six Sigma, a tradition-

1 *A Whole New Mind*, Pink, Daniel
2 *Creating a Customer-Centered Culture*, Lawton, Robin
3 *The Creative Age*, Cohen, Gene D.
4 Rosenfeld *Making the Invisible, Visible*, Robert Rosenfeld
5 *The Whole Brain Business Book*, by creative thinking pioneer, Ned Herrmann

ally left-brain tool, offers enormous potential for right-brain thinkers. Strategic use of Six Sigma means using the tools and methods, as appropriate, to address the pressing needs of the organization. When Six Sigma first started, it was focused on the pressing needs of the time: quality and cost reduction. Now, as more organizations have achieved higher quality levels and lower costs, the pressing need has become Innovation. Six Sigma can be used to address this need as well. The front end of Innovation is creativity and idea generation; this is predominantly right-brain thinking. Addressing Innovation with Six Sigma means embracing the traditional left-brain Six Sigma methods and using them to address right-brain opportunities. By using Six Sigma in this way, Innovation is enabled by bridging the gap between the right and left hemispheres of the brain. I call this the *Innovation Gap,* the gap between right-brain creativity and left-brain execution. We must bridge the Innovation Gap if we are to turn ideas into reality. If used appropriately, the Six Sigma methodology accelerates Innovation and enables growth by providing methods and tools to bridge the Innovation Gap. A key feature of this book is to show leaders how to do this.

As the world shrinks, I have started to realize that "best in class" and even "world-class" is no longer good enough to be successful in the Creative Age. We all need to take our personal and business performance to out-of-this-world, stratospheric levels of success.

Organizations are being challenged all the time to do more with less, yet if you ask the members of these organizations whether they feel they are encouraged or even allowed to fulfill their potential, they will probably say no.[6] Organizations seem to be afraid to encourage their best people to leave their comfort zones. Six Sigma can help deal with this paradox as we use it as a key enabler in achieving balance. As Zig Zigler tells us in *See You at the Top,* it is time to bravely leave our zone of comfort and enter the zone of effectiveness.

I have heard several experts claim that Six Sigma is a luxury that is affordable only for larger organizations. But Six Sigma is far from being a luxury. The return on investment is exceptional. Another common myth is that Six Sigma stifles Innovation because of the

6   *The 8th Habit, Covey, Stephen*

strong focus on data, logic, and analysis. This can be true, but only when Six Sigma addresses only the What and the How. When used to enable business success by addressing the strategic needs of the organization (the Why), Six Sigma is both impressive and effective. If Innovation is high on the organization's strategic agenda, then Six Sigma can enable Innovation. In fact, Innovation and Six Sigma can and should enable each other. Any organization trying to stay ahead of the game by sustaining, improving, and growing will benefit from both Six Sigma and Innovation.

I'm not foolish enough to claim that Innovation needs Six Sigma any more or less than other management techniques. What I do urge you to consider is that strategic use of Six Sigma can help make organizations better at Innovation. Successful integration of Six Sigma and Innovation depends on the balance between the What, How, and Why. *The Balanced Innovator* explains how an affordable Six Sigma program, integrated with Innovation, can be used effectively by organizations of all sizes. *The Balanced Innovator* will help you achieve the What, How, Why Balance.

The Burning Platform—Case for Action

Does your organization or business have a *burning platform*—a real need to take action on something that is stopping you from being as successful as you should be? Perhaps your profit levels are too low, or your costs are too high. Maybe your quality isn't as good as you and your customers would like it to be. You may even have a combination of issues that compound the problem. It is probable that some of the following questions are troubling your leadership right now.

- » How can we grow our business?
- » Why do we consistently lose business to our competitors?
- » Why is our creativity stifled?
- » Why are we forever fighting fires and don't have time to be innovative?
- » Why do our creative ideas seem to dissipate without ever becoming reality?
- » We seem to be on the threshold of something great, so why can't we get there?

If any of these questions resonated with you, then you have taken the first step by recognizing that there is an issue. Here's the good news: you can address the issue, and it won't be as difficult as you may think. By balancing the What, How, and Why of your strategy, business models, and projects, you can take your organization to the next level and beyond. Achieving the What, How, Why Balance is within your grasp.

I have based the ideas, patterns, and thoughts in *The Balanced Innovator* on more than thirty years of business development and program management experience and many years of extensive research. Experience that includes leading sales, marketing, and business development campaigns that have brought in over $2.5 billion in revenue for the companies represented. Experience and knowledge that includes; designing, developing, and delivering a thought-provoking training program to several hundred students on Six Sigma, Innovation, and growth. Experience gained while traveling to more than thirty countries around the world, as well as to most of the United States. Experience and knowledge that translates into a few simple yet key concepts that supplement and build on traditional management and leadership programs; such as Six Sigma, in an easy-to-understand way. You can start applying these ideas the same day you read about them.

The Balanced Innovator explains how achieving the What, How, Why Balance with methods like Six Sigma can help you be more successful. It clarifies how Six Sigma, Innovation, and Growth are inextricably linked, with each complementing the other. *The Balanced Innovator* will introduce a few new ideas, such as:

» Balanced Innovation.
» How to bridge the Innovation Gap.
» Understanding who has the power in the Chorus of the Customer.
» The chorus is everywhere and always.
» Business Development is an activity and not just a departments' name.
» Everybody is responsible for growth.

You will also learn key concepts:

- » How to hurdle the barriers that get in your way.
- » How to love the customer and prove it through your values and behaviors.
- » How to irrelevantize the competition by focusing on the critical areas that make a difference, rather than obsessing about a competitor.
- » How to unparalyze the paradigm by challenging your thoughts to enable more creativity.

You will also find areas where you can use a variety of business tools, including a simple technique called *The 5-D Methodology*. The 5-D method simplifies traditional Six Sigma programs by ensuring that data is quickly and effectively turned into usable information; it does this by balancing data with intuition. The 5-D method allows fast, knowledge-based decisions to be made that turn ideas into reality as soon as possible.

At the end of each chapter, you will find a summary of the key points and a few "so what" questions to help you place the thoughts into context.

Why *The Balanced Innovator?*

Many business books today are full of insightful observations and thoughts—for example, *The Purple Cow* by Seth Godin, *Blue Ocean Strategy* by W. Chan Kim and Renée Mauborgne, and *The World Is Flat* by Thomas Friedman. There is also an abundance of books describing continuous improvement and Six Sigma. (See *Strategic Six Sigma* by Dick Smith and Jerry Blakeslee; and *The Six Sigma Black Belt Handbook* by Tom McCarty, Lorraine Daniels, Michael Bremer, and Praveen Gupta. So what does *The Balanced Innovator* offer that these other books do not?

The Balanced Innovator provides the missing link between right-brain creativity and left-brain discipline. It shares personal experiences that you will be able to relate to and practical advice that you will be able to apply to your everyday challenges. Even more exciting, the ideas and principles are easy to understand and use. *The Balanced Innovator* provides the link between what is and what should be.

Where else could you find a Purple Cow swimming in a Blue Ocean at the edge of the Flat World? If you use the power of your imagination for a moment, I'm sure you can visualize a green elephant flying through the blue sky to out-of-this-world levels of success.

I want my children and my children's children to grow and develop in a healthy society with a thriving economy. I want them to live in an environment that has tremendous opportunity for both personal and societal development and achievement. My dream can come true only if organizations are as successful as they can possibly be, focused on their customers, clients, guests, and other partners. This relentless focus on an increasingly demanding customer base will lead to customer success through higher-quality products and services. Consequently, customer success will lead to business growth. It is vital, therefore, that Innovation is focused on creating and adding value to both our existing customers and potential new ones.

I have written *The Balanced Innovator* to help you succeed. Everybody should have access to success because success is contagious! The more success there is, the more success is generated; the more success being generated, the more success there is. Moreover, success leads to a healthy society and growing economy.

The Balanced Innovator is intended to give you hope and invigorate your passion—two essential ingredients for successful Innovation. Essentially, it is about taking your success to the next level. *The Balanced Innovator* can help you take ownership of your success. Ownership and attitude are two of the most important factors that have helped me be successful. They can help make you successful, too! If you take ownership, exert passion, have a positive, can-do attitude, and then apply the ideas and methods found in this book, you are well on your way to those out-of-this-world levels of success. You are on your way to achieving the What, How, Why Balance.

If writing this book makes a positive difference to just one company and less than ten individuals, then I have made a worthwhile contribution. But what if hundreds of companies and tens of thousands of individuals are positively affected? What if their performance soars as a result? That is the contagious impact of success. So go spread the word. Good luck on your journey.

chapter 1

what is innovation?

Innovation

Innovation is so vogue in business language today that it is almost a fashion. Try to Google or Yahoo the word *Innovation,* and you will be amazed at the number of entries you will find. Everybody is talking about Innovation. Every company claims to be innovative, and to prove the point, there are more conferences on Innovation than the average ninja can shake a black belt at. So I asked myself a simple question: What the *bleep* is Innovation? Is it a verb or a noun? Is it an input or an output, or is it the process? Is Innovation imagination, inspiration, ideation, invention, creation, or improvisation? It certainly takes dedication and usually lots of perspiration! I believe that Innovation is the result of all of these things. We all know that Innovation is good, as long as it adds value in some way. It can be continuous (i.e., the progressive improvement of something) or discontinuous (i.e., the introduction of something new that takes away the need or desire for the thing it replaces). This can be a product or a service, and it can happen in every walk of life.

Most people would agree that Innovation is exciting and groundbreaking (hence, the more than 120 million Internet search results). There is no doubt that Innovation is one of the keys to growth, and everybody is rightly concerned about growth, especially revenue growth. So where does Innovation occur? Why is Innovation so important, and what type of organizations are innovative? The catalyst for Innovation is multifaceted; it can be fear, confusion, conflict, or desperation. Innovation may be triggered by loss of market share, by breakthrough technology, or simply by luck. Let's talk about luck for a moment. Luck is best described as when opportunity meets preparedness.[1] If you are prepared and you recognize the opportunity when it presents itself, the Innovation has started. The key to Innovation is need or desire. So is Innovation an art or a science?

The Innovation Gap

People who predominantly use the right side of their brains are the thinkers, the dreamers, the artisans, the poets, and the storytellers. They have dreams and throw out ideas in abundance. They are the folks known as out-of-the-box thinkers. Right-brain thinkers try to solve unknown problems by immersing themselves in the big picture. They find luck by being prepared for opportunity when it presents itself. On the other hand, people who predominantly use the left side of their brains prefer to solve known problems. They are logical and analytical and make tactical execution their priority. They are the program managers, the accountants, and the engineers who love to stay inside the box. Left-brain thinkers often talk about out-of-the-box thinking, but they are usually jumping from one box and into another. (More about that confounded box in chapter 7.) Left-brain thinkers use luck by turning the opportunity into reality. So where does Innovation fit? Innovation is the art, science, or other act of introducing something new that adds value. Innovation eliminates the box and bridges the gap between the right and left hemispheres of the brain. As I explained in the introduction, I call this gap the Innovation Gap. Innovation turns dreams and ideas into reality by bridging that gap. If the Innovation Gap isn't bridged, the idea is merely a dream.

Balanced Innovation

"But growth is about Innovation and creativity in developing new technologies through science," an engineering friend of mine stated recently. "More to the point, it's the engineers and scientists who

---

1   *Lead the Field,* Earl Nightingale

really drive growth!" My response was both yes and no. Engineers and scientists can and do drive growth and are often innovators, but they don't have a monopoly on the subject. Many engineers and scientists find it difficult to construct a sentence containing the word Innovation, unless it also contains either science, technology, or engineering. Science, technology, and engineering are the intellectual aspects of Innovation that can also be described as What we do.

There are also the emotional aspects of Innovation. Innovation, as we have discussed, must add value, and if there is no or limited emotional connection with our customers, then the value will be limited at best. Think about the way good storytelling plays on human emotions and behaviors. A great invention on its own isn't necessarily Innovation, especially if it adds no value at that particular point in time. Storytelling is a way of explaining how the solution works in a way that connects emotionally with the client.

What about behaviors? The correct behaviors tend toward positive emotional connections, both internally and externally with our customers and other partners. Strong, positive emotional connections lead to optimism. Optimistic organizations have been found to innovate much more successfully than pessimistic ones. (For more information on the role of optimism in Innovation, see *Putting Hope to Work* by Harry Hutson and Barbara Perry.) The emotional, behavioral, and storytelling aspects of Innovation are the human factors and can also be described as Why we do things.

Innovation is necessary everywhere and can occur anywhere. Innovation is not reserved for the domain of the scientist. For example, Innovation occurs in organizations in places like the finance department, in the contracts and legal departments, and throughout the supply chain. Think about the way a lawyer justifies her fees; that's Innovation through storytelling in its finest form. (To any lawyers, that's a joke!) On a more serious note, the Dell business model is an excellent example of organizational Innovation. The way Dell introduced build-to-order capabilities through the innovative use of the supply chain and contracting methods gave the company a significant competitive edge. Dell's business model allowed customers to quickly order and pay for the computer they wanted, rather than buying off-the-shelf computers that usually included many software programs that were neither wanted nor asked for. Their effective and innovative use of the supply chain meant that their inventory levels and costs were significantly lower than traditional manufacturers'. It made them different. Dell's technology was no better than the incumbents of the time, but their success from startup to industry leader was phenomenal.

In addition to the formal organizations such as the supply chain, it is often the informal connections within organizations that enable the Innovation to thrive. These social networks connect the dots between individuals and organizations who collectively add value, a process known as using *social capital*. Social capital refers to the wealth of managers' or leaders' relationships within and beyond the organization. Social capital focuses on the value a leader or manager adds through his or her relationships with other people. Using social capital can be a key enabler. Where you don't have social capital, borrow somebody else's. These formal and informal organizational aspects can also be described as How we do things.

Six Sigma Black Belts, the expert practitioners of continuous improvement methods, are often members of the best-connected social networks in an organization. Don't be afraid to borrow the social capital of your Black Belts. (For a more complete description of the term *Six Sigma Black Belt,* see chapter 2.)

The Venn diagram in figure 1.1 shows how balanced Innovation works. Notice how the intellectual, organizational, and human factors are equally important. In other words, What we do, How we do it, and Why we do it are equally important. You will also see that the factors are all interconnected, suggesting that successful Innovation is dependent on balance.

Your intellectual strength shows that you have the capabilities to deliver the product or service that your customers need. It is about your core competencies. Your organizational strength shows that you have the ability to produce what your customers need. Your human strengths show that you understand the needs, that you empathize with your customers, and that you are focused on satisfying those needs. Your behaviors prove that you can be trusted and the way you communicate proves that you are in empathy. Each factor validates the others. The human factors validate the intellectual and organiza-

what is innovation?

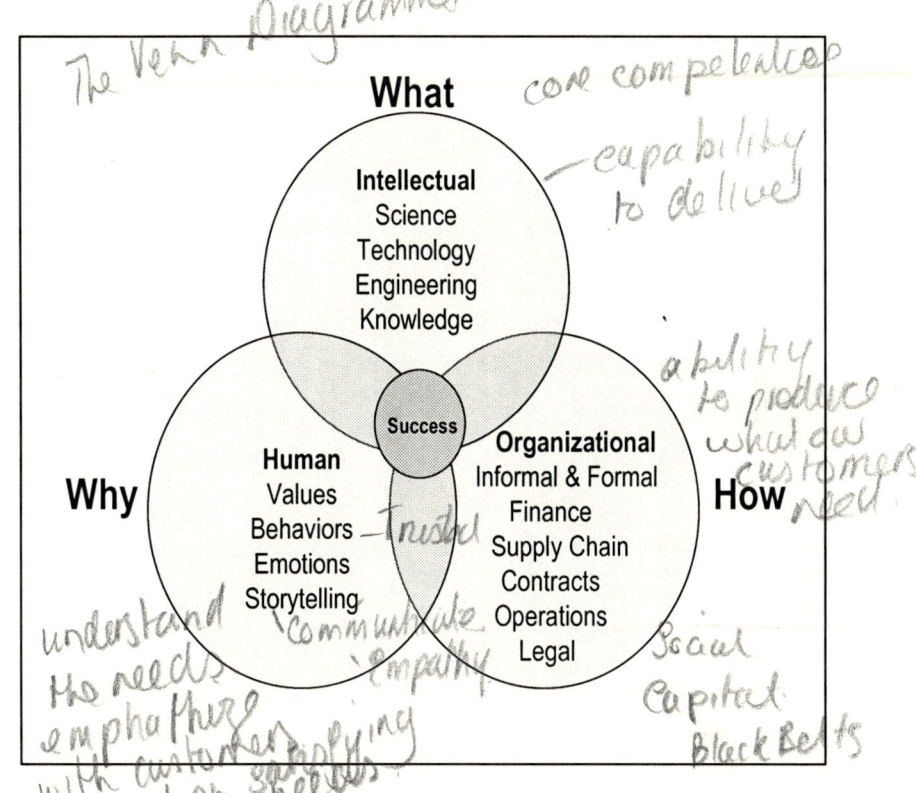

Figure 1.1. Balanced Innovation

tional, the intellectual factors validate the organizational and human, and the organizational factors validate the human and intellectual. So the What validates the How and Why, and vice versa. This is defined as the *What, How, Why Balance*. As I mentioned in the introduction, this What, How, Why Balance is a key feature of *The Balanced Innovator* and will be used throughout the book. In order to achieve success in anything we do, we must reach a minimum threshold in each of the intellectual, organizational, and human factors. If one of these factors is weak, the What, How, and Why are not balanced.

Unfortunately, many organizations are focused more on one area at the expense of another, like those shown in figure 1.2 (next page).

Unbalanced Innovation occurs when Innovation is focused on one factor at the expense of the others. In example A, the Innovation is highly intellectual, focused on the technical aspects but not necessarily focused on customer needs and certainly not focused on

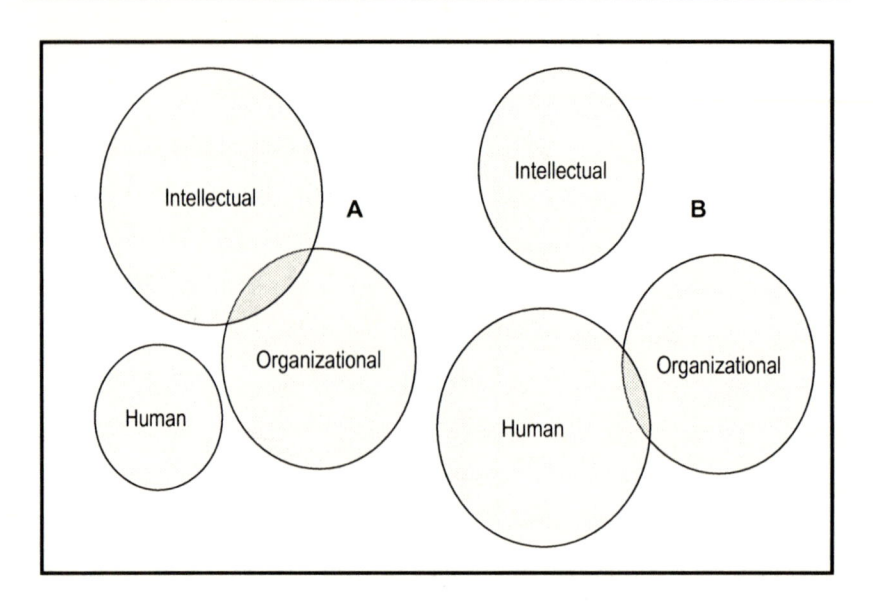

Figure 1.2. Unbalanced Innovation

telling the story to make the right emotional connection. Think of the Betamax videotape system. Betamax was regarded by many as technically superior to the VHS system but was a comparative commercial failure. Had the Betamax tape manufacturers adopted a more balanced approach and focused on the organizational and human factors of Innovation as well as the intellectual ones, there may have been an entirely different outcome. In example B, the story may be compelling but the solution may have little substance. This type of imbalance is usually seen in organizations that have outstanding marketing and business development professionals, but their focus is all about winning new business rather than on execution. Their success is usually short lived. Contrast this again with figure 1.1, where all three factors are equally important. Companies that exhibit out-of-this-world performance have a balanced approach to Innovation.

You can find a good example of balanced Innovation at Disney theme parks. Disney parks don't have the highest or fastest rides, and they are among the world's most expensive parks to visit. Yet they are by far the most widely recognized, most frequently visited, and most commercially successful. This is because Disney places importance on the total experience. The way they tell the story and the way they make it easy for you to visit their parks is just as important as the excitement of the rides. Disney doesn't want its guests spending a lot of time waiting in line. They have pioneered Fastpass, which allows guests to book ride times in advance to minimize waiting time. Disney recognizes that the more time the guests spend in line, the less time they are walking past those enticing vendors—not to mention the frustration and boredom incurred. If a line is inevitable, Disney will find ways to entertain guests until they reach the attraction, usually by introducing a story to build the guests anticipation of the ride. This makes the experience even more compelling, enhancing those positive emotional connections. Disney may not have a Six Sigma program, but it does have a balanced approach to Innovation.

I shared the concept of balanced and unbalanced Innovation with an audience at a conference recently and one participant asked, "What if you have an unbalanced model, but it matches the needs and expectations of your customers?" The question floored me for a second, and then I realized that the unbalanced Innovation may match the expectations of existing customers, but this is probably disabling growth in a macro or overall market sense. In chapter 8 we will look at growth in detail, but for now I will say that even if our unbalanced approach to Innovation does match our current customer base, we are not looking at ways to find new customers for our offerings or new solutions for existing customers and certainly not new offerings for new customers. In other words, unbalanced innovation forces us to concentrate our existing offerings on our existing customers. It is also the reason why many organizations get trapped in their comfort zones.

The ideas behind balanced and unbalanced Innovation are equally applicable to strategies, business models, and organic growth. A good strategy is one that reflects the larger external market or macro environment as well as the micro needs of the specific market segment. A good business model is one that enables the strategy. Organizations that match their business models and strategies to the needs of the external environment are more likely to grow organically—that is, they increase revenue through the acquisition of new business. Organic growth is achieved by winning new business.

I have conducted research across business sectors such as retail, high tech, manufacturing, and service, and I have analyzed more than thirty major new business proposals; my results all show that proposals offering balanced solutions and balanced Innovations always win against unbalanced proposals.

You are also trying to make it as easy as possible for the customer to do business with you. Having a balanced strategy and business model, including a balanced approach to Innovation, is essential if companies have ambitions to move to the next level and achieve out-of-this-world success.

Achieving the What, How, Why Balance doesn't necessarily mean that all three factors are equal, but it does mean that the weakest factor must reach a minimum threshold. The interconnections and validations are essential. If there is little or no validation between one factor and another, the intersection is weak and the What, How, Why Balance is compromised. Without this balance, success is limited. The strength of the central interconnection between the intellectual, organizational, and human factors dictates the likelihood of success.

In the next chapter, I will provide some background on Six Sigma.

Key Points in Chapter 1

> » The Innovation Gap needs to be bridged to turn creative ideas into reality.
> » The key to success is finding the right balance between the intellectual, organizational, and human factors—the What, How, Why Balance.
> » Successful companies exhibit the What, How, Why Balance.
> » An unbalanced approach is likely to force organizations into strategies aimed purely at existing customers with existing products.
> » In a shrinking world that increasingly emphasizes growth, business leaders are looking for help.

Key Questions to Ask Yourself

> » Are you an innovative company? Explain.
> » Is your Innovation balanced? Describe your reasons.
> » How do you match your Innovation to the opportunities in the macro environment of the wider marketplace?

chapter 2

some background on six sigma

Six Sigma has been about continuous improvement. If you have been in business for any amount of time, you will probably recognize Six Sigma as one of the most widely used quality-improvement methods available today. In my opinion, it goes much further than that. Six Sigma is one of the most important strategic management initiatives of recent times and is well established in many industries, from banking to high-tech engineering. Six Sigma is now so well recognized that it has found its way into the curriculum of many universities. Despite this wide recognition, Six Sigma is still in its infancy. Six Sigma professionals still embrace the needs of left-brain thinkers while generally ignoring Innovation; they immerse themselves in tactics rather than strategy. It is time for Six Sigma to be taken to the next level. Successful Six Sigma programs have the right What, How, Why Balance.

A Quick History Lesson and Definition

The origins of Six Sigma date back to the 1980s, when Motorola developed an improvement program to help fight back from the constant battering they received from Japan. Many Japanese companies were gaining significant market share in the United States and other markets. Motorola used Six Sigma to track quality while ensuring that product performance met customer requirements.

Sigma (σ) represents a unit of measurement that calculates the spread about the mean average of a process. Therefore, the higher the Sigma level, the less variation and fewer defects the process will have. In its purest definition, Six Sigma is the statistical standard of excellence, where only 3.4 defects per 1 million opportunities will occur.

There are many continuous-improvement initiatives linked with Six Sigma, such as Lean and even Lean Six Sigma. In their most common definitions, Lean makes a process faster and Six Sigma makes a process better. For this book I am using the term Six Sigma in the global sense, as a methodology that also encompasses Lean techniques in a total business excellence methodology. In fact, many of the companies using Six Sigma today sought out the best practices of earlier initiatives (e.g., Quality Circles, Total Quality Management (TQM), Business Process Reengineering (BPR), and Just in Time) and added change management and cultural aspects into the design of their Six Sigma program. As I mentioned in the introduction, the main purpose of this book is to share with you the importance of balance and how this can be achieved through the link between Six Sigma, Innovation, and growth. One of my goals is to help to stretch your thinking beyond the traditional use of Six Sigma by taking it to the next level. This next level is what I am calling Six Sigma for Innovation.

The Big Picture

To explain the strategic use of Six Sigma, I'd like to borrow from a story I first heard told by Harvey Mackay, a motivational speaker and the author of *Swim with the Sharks Without Being Eaten Alive* and *Beware the Naked Man Who Offers You His Shirt*.

A fast-moving entrepreneurial company had just hired a vice president of Six Sigma to take the program to the next level and complement the tremendous success of their Lean Efficiency team. The vice president was a keen classical music fan and had acquired a pair of tickets to attend a live performance of Schubert's Unfinished Symphony. Unfortunately, he had to leave town at the last moment and so gave the tickets to the director of lean efficiency. On his return he was eager to hear how much his new friend had enjoyed the show. The director told him, "For considerable periods of time, the four oboe players were not playing their instruments; their work could have easily been covered by other members of the orchestra. On several occasions, the twelve violin players were all playing the same notes; this duplication of effort could have been considerably reduced. If the intent was to have higher volume, this could have been achieved by the use of amplifiers. I saw no reason why the brass section repeated a part of the score that had already been played by the strings. In fact, this two-hour performance could easily have been completed in half the time, and if Schubert would have been more efficient, he may have actually completed the symphony after all."

The lesson here is about seeing the big picture rather than focusing on the tactics. It is about effectiveness rather than efficiencies, and it is about understanding the needs of the customer. That is where Six Sigma should focus: creating and delivering the right solutions to meet customer needs. Six Sigma must focus on the Why as well as on the What and the How.

Some General Background

A *Black Belt* is a full-time practitioner of Six Sigma. Black Belts undergo several weeks of training (usually between four and six, depending on the program) and lead several projects before presenting one of their projects to a board for certification. *Green Belts* are part-time practitioners. Green Belt training is fundamental in nature and less arduous than Black Belt training. Unlike Black Belts, Green Belts usually stay in their regular jobs and use Six Sigma tools and methods to enable success in their everyday activities.

Some organizations employ *Master Black Belts,* who usually have several years' experience in the field and have been through many cycles of learning. A Master Black Belt will normally coach and mentor several Black Belts and should have a close working relationship with the senior leadership in the organization.

Companies using Six Sigma are shouting to the world that they are committed to delivering high-quality products, services, and solutions. Six Sigma is used to eliminate waste, reduce variation, and improve efficiencies. Customers and shareholders alike are delighted by these virtues. Evidence suggests, though, that as noble and important as these efforts may be, they are internally focused.

For Six Sigma to continue to make a significant contribution to success, it has to be at the heart of the strategy of the organization. It must be championed by leadership, welcomed by management, and embraced as part of the culture. The workforce will use it on a daily basis as the way the organization solves problems. How do you get this buy-in? I suggest you prove the value of the program to the key stakeholders.

Figure 2.1 shows how Six Sigma has evolved over the years. As Six Sigma becomes part of the DNA of a department or other function of an organization, contemporary leaders will find new areas to deploy it. Initial deployment was all about productivity—reducing debt and freeing up cash. Soon companies were using Six Sigma to reduce the variation in processes and improve program performance overall.

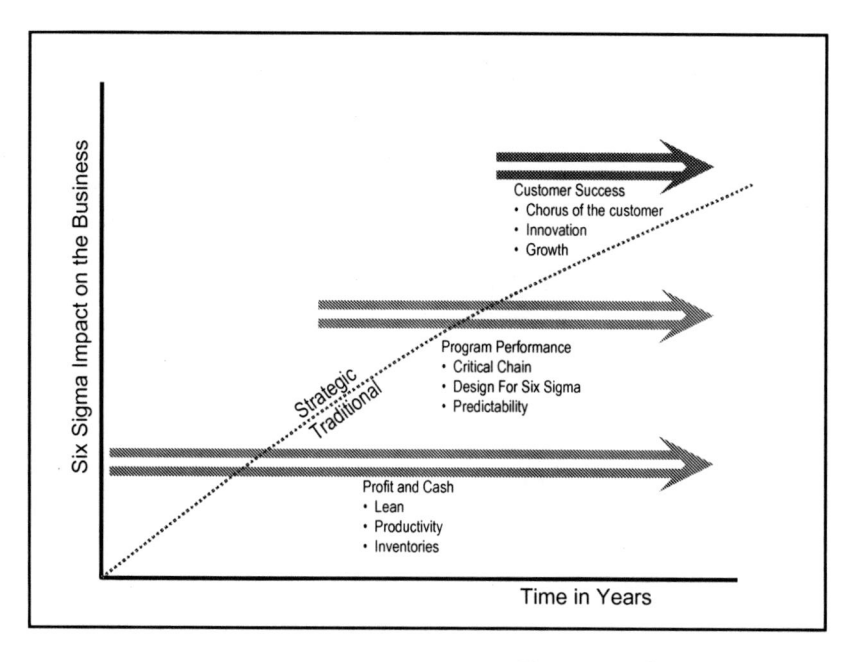

Figure 2.1. The Impact of Six Sigma; y = f(x)

Through Six Sigma, companies such as Raytheon, Bank of America, GE, Honeywell, Xerox, Cummings, and Motorola have been able to reduce costs and add value to the Annual Operating Plan (AOP). (For more details on this subject, see iSixSigma's January 2007 magazine article *Six Sigma Saves a Fortune*.[1]) These Fortune 500 companies have mainly achieved savings through improved efficien-

---

1   http://www.isixsigma-magazine.com

cies, eliminating waste, removing duplication of effort, and reducing variation. The annual reports of these companies testify that productivity has improved and program performance is getting better. Although these leading-edge firms recognize that they must continue to improve productivity and performance, there is a growing understanding that there may be more for Six Sigma to contribute.

As you can see in figure 2.1, *yes,* there is more! Once the corporate belt tightening has been achieved—defects reduced and processes lean and efficient—Six Sigma can and should be used to address the new and emerging strategic needs. For example, companies can use Six Sigma to enable both Innovation and Growth with staggering results. In effect, Six Sigma is being taken to the next level, but so far, only on rare occasions.

The industry standard for the Six Sigma method is shown in figure 2.2:*DMAIC,*[2] or Define, Measure, Analyze, Improve, and Control.

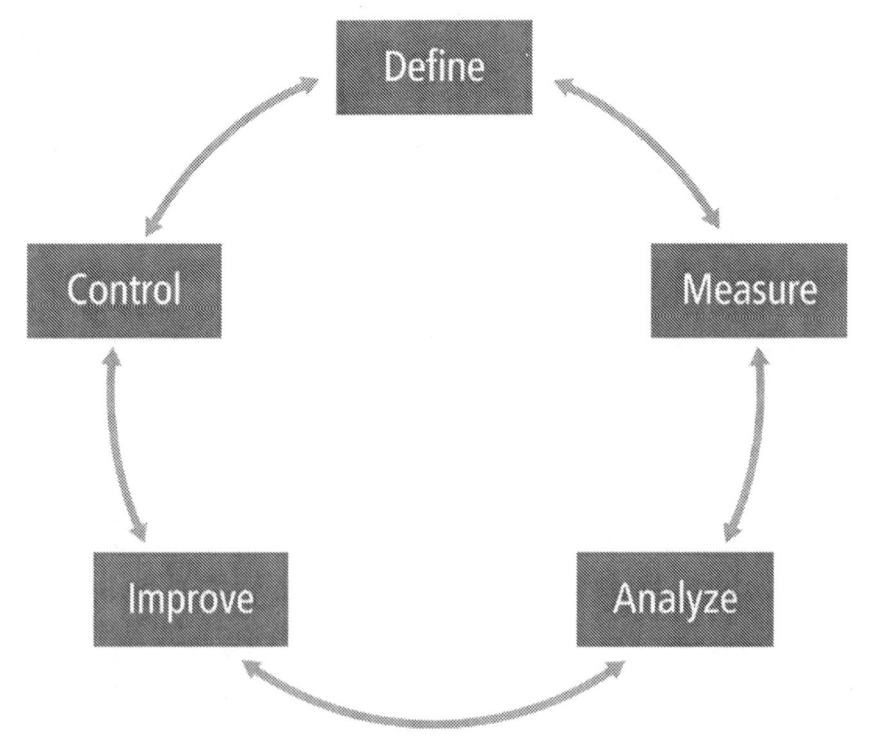

Figure 2.2. The DMAIC Six Sigma Method

2   *The Breakthrough Approach* ,Introduced by Mikel Harry and Richard Schroeder

Define is the visioning stage of the process, where problems are recognized and opportunities for improvement are identified. This can be simple but will more likely be complex. The root cause of the problem is almost always process related, which can be difficult for some people to accept. In a recent blog on his website, author Seth Godin said it very well: "If process makes you nervous, it's probably because it threatens your reliance on intuition. Get over it. The best processes leverage your intuition and give it room to thrive." However, I will add that if a process is broken, it needs to be fixed. No amount of leaning out a process to make it more efficient will help if the process ultimately isn't fixed. The methods and tools of Six Sigma are the best available to help fix broken processes. Some managers struggle to define the problem because they see it as undermining their positions; they feel they should know the answers. Help them out of the dark ages, please—or as Seth says, "Get over it!" Let the data lead you toward knowledge-based decisions.

The **measure** and **analyze** phases are at the center of the problem-solving process. In effect, during these phases is where the problem and its root causes get characterized and where the relationship between the key variables and process outputs becomes focused, otherwise known as our old friend, $y = f(x)$. A solid root-cause analysis methodology can be worth its weight in gold.

The **improve** phase is where the solutions identified earlier in the process are implemented and measured. During the **control** phase Black Belts establish accountability, metrics, and controls that help to sustain success and the implementation of the improved process once they have moved on to the next shiny problem.

Six Sigma professionals are the kings and queens of data, but data can be daunting. We need to convert data into information so that we can help our leaders make knowledge-based decisions. This is even truer at the front end of business—the area traditionally deemed the domain of sales, marketing, and business development. Coping with rapid and continuous change in competitive markets is one of the biggest challenges facing business leaders today. The speed of change is increasing. Innovation is a must. Today's luxury, once experienced, becomes the necessity of tomorrow. (To illustrate this point, my six-year-old daughter Lexi recently announced that she needs a new TV in her bedroom because the picture quality is poor. She was comparing it to the new plasma TV we have in the family room! When I was her age we had one TV with three channels, and it was in black and white—and at the time, I loved it!)

For organizations to grow, they need to focus on their customers. I have witnessed many great companies prove that relentless customer focus leads to customer success, and customer success leads to growth. It is often said in pharmaceuticals that if you focus on the people, the profits will follow. Most companies acknowledge this, even including "customer focus" in their mission statements, but do they truly live by this creed? Are these companies truly externally focused? Six Sigma can help create success for our customers, but how can Six Sigma help, you may well ask? We will address this in the next chapter.

Key Points in Chapter 2

» Six Sigma has to remain contemporary by focusing on the organization's strategic needs.
» Successful Six Sigma programs and projects exhibit the What, How, Why Balance.
» Six Sigma started as a strategic initiative to ensure continuous improvement.
» Once the requisite belt tightening has been achieved, Six Sigma should be refocused to address the next strategic needs of the organization.

Key Questions to Ask Yourself

» Do you have a passion for continuous improvement?
» Do you have a Six Sigma program?
    o If not, why not?
    o If yes, is it part of the organization's culture?
        • What benefits do you see in a Six Sigma program?
        • What is the downside to having a Six Sigma program?

chapter 3

innovation and six sigma

As suggested earlier, Six Sigma should be about addressing the big picture. By focusing on Innovation and Growth, Six Sigma can enable organizations to achieve their strategic goals. Six Sigma for Innovation is embryonic, and its path is still being defined. Six Sigma for Innovation and Growth isn't just about being more efficient in your use of discretionary budgets[1]; it is about increasing the effectiveness of your organization by doing the right things. Six Sigma provides focus, speed, agility, discipline, "honest broker" leadership, and facilitation by the use of proven tools, techniques, and methods. With Six Sigma, many organizations like Raytheon, GE, and Honeywell have become more efficient, improved their program performance, and made their operations leaner. I have used the same methods and techniques at the front end of business, with great effect and I encourage you to do the same.

There are dozens of books on Six Sigma, and I won't get into the heavy details here. (See; *Strategic Six Sigma* by Dick Smith and Jerry Blakeslee; and *The Six Sigma Black Belt Handbook* by Tom McCarty, Lorraine Daniels, Michael Bremer, and Praveen Gupta). I would like to take the basic DMAIC method shown in figure 2.2 and look at how it works when the constraint to success is external to the organization—for example, the customer's ability to buy, or the impact of competition. This can seriously affect revenue growth and is where Innovation is very important. Consider the double-loop learning diagram shown in figure 3.1.

---

1 Budgets set aside from profit to spend on advancing the organization in areas such as research and development and other new business investments.

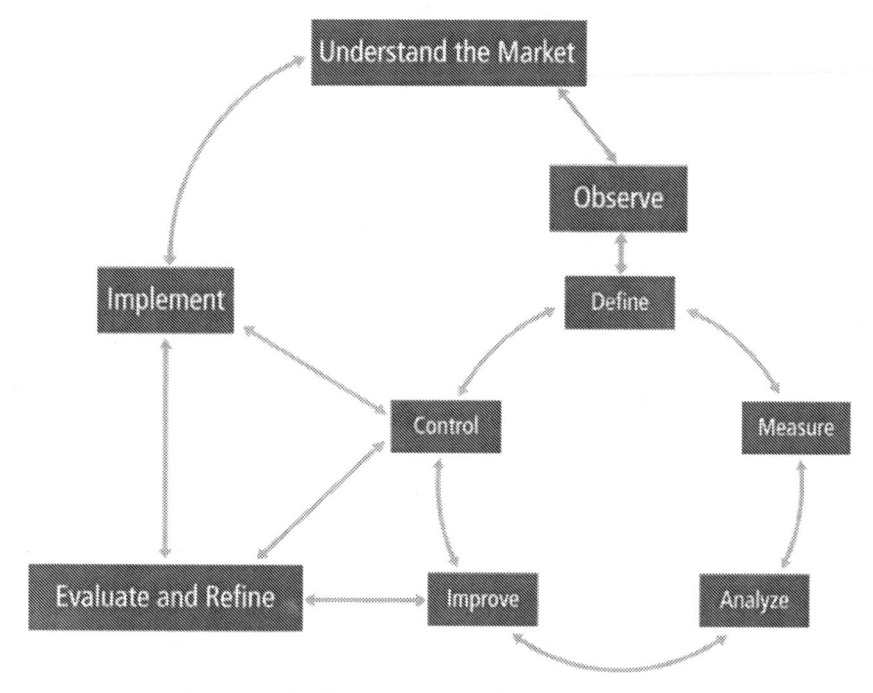

Fig. 3.1. Six Sigma and Double-Loop Learning

The outer loop represents the external environment. To understand the market, we need competitive intelligence and customer intelligence. We need to know what the perceptions are, where the disruptive technology may be coming from, and what the constraints are (for example, limited funding, early in-service requirements, and so on). By **understanding the market**, we are taking a macro look at the general trends and movements in the marketplace. In addition, noncompetitive intelligence can provide valuable insight into the market environment and what your customers might expect in terms of the level of service. Noncompetitive intelligence is information about organizations that your customers will be aware of or even intimate with but that are not in direct competition with you. For example, your customers may also be the customers of companies like Disney and Dell. They will expect you to treat them as well as these other organizations treat them. Companies like Disney and Dell could be setting expectations way beyond what your immediate industry standard delivers, so you need to be aware of what those standards are.

The **observe** phase takes a micro look at specific market segments and customers and is closely linked with **understanding the market**; the two phases will most likely be iterative, with each phase confirming and reconfirming the other. This is the observation of real people in real life—what makes them tick, what confuses them, what keeps them awake, what motivates them. It is the art of ethnography in action. *Ethnography* is defined in Webster's dictionary as the branch of anthropology that provides scientific description of human societies; in other words, it is the anthropology of groups and is very informative when used in the workplace. Once we have a good handle on these external issues, we can look for opportunities and go into the **define** phase of the DMAIC Six Sigma method. In this model, the visioning is focused on opportunities to satisfy the needs of the external environment. Once we have been through the **measure** and **analyze** phases, we have developed a solution and started the **improve** phase; we should test the idea. Go back into the external environment, and evaluate and refine as necessary. Don't get too attached to the implementation because every idea can be made better! Get internal and external feedback—after all, this is the **improve** phase. Establish real results, and then put in place the **controls** to help manage the environment to make best use of the outcome from the project.

Bridging the Innovation Gap with Six Sigma

So if Six Sigma is about bridging the gap between what is and what should be, and Innovation bridges the gap between the right and left sides of the brain, then Six Sigma and Innovation are linked. Both start with an understanding of the current state, then you visualize the desired future state, and then you find an appropriate way to get there. Both create and deliver value—one by solving problems and the other by introducing something new. So the inputs and outputs may be different, but the methodology is similar. Therefore, Six Sigma can be used as a key enabler for Innovation. Six Sigma professionals have been explaining that it is all about reducing variation, eliminating waste, improving quality, and reducing costs—all incredibly noble and important! So Six Sigma has been all about the left side of the brain; it is very process oriented, with variation as the enemy.

Let's think about this for a moment: why should the left-brain thinkers have all the fun? (Now there's a concept for a cocktail hour discussion!) So what happens when Six Sigma is applied by those of us who are more oriented to the right sides of our brains? Six Sigma then becomes an art as well as a science. I know from experience that when applied to the right side of the brain in addition to the left side, Six Sigma provides even more potential. That potential starts to be realized when you bridge the Innovation Gap, which you'll remember is the gap between right-brain creativity and left-brain delivery.

Innovation is said to embrace variation, but this is true only at the front end of creativity and idea generation. Once ideas have been generated, a selection process is needed to identify the critical few that will make a difference. Six Sigma tools such as decision trees (see description in the Appendix to this book) can help this selection process. In other words, Six Sigma methods can help turn right-brain creativity into left-brain delivery.

When looking for team members for a project, you could aim for diversity by recruiting a mix of right-brain and left-brain thinkers. It's amazing how this simple tactic can drive the Innovation toward balance; the difference in opinion and thought process helps validate the team members across the What, How, and Why behind the project.

Where Six Sigma Plays

In my experience, I have found eight areas where Six Sigma can enable growth through customer success (see figure 3.2). These areas are where Six Sigma makes a positive difference, in both the external and internal loops of the double-loop process shown in figure 3.1.

The box covering repeatable and reliable processes is where Six Sigma traditionally contributes. The other eight boxes represent areas where Six Sigma can be used to enable customer success and therefore growth. Notice how everything is focused on the customer? The customer is the center of the universe, and the flow goes both ways. We listen to our customers, and we provide solutions for our customers. By connecting emotionally, we are able to understand their needs, develop solutions to meet those needs, and tell our story in a simple-

```
                    Six Sigma
                 Repeatable and
                 Reliable Processes
   Identifying    = Productivity      Customer
Customer Needs                        Engagement

With the Customer                     Growth
 For the Customer      The            Diagnosis
                     Customer
   Increasing                         Defining
Customer Success                      Solution

Partnering Through                    Increasing
 the Value Chain                      Program Capture
```

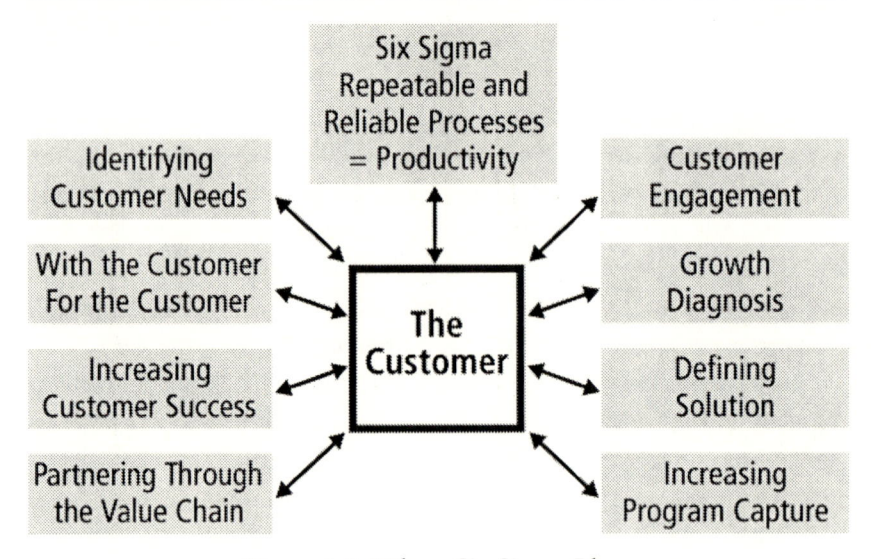

Figure 3.2. Where Six Sigma Plays

to-understand way. We are truly in empathy with our customers. Our goal should be to partner with our customers. Following is a short explanation of each of the focus areas.

Identifying Customer Needs. Hold a facilitated workshop or series of activities to help a diverse and disparate customer base arrive at a common vision, need, and goal. Use Six Sigma tools and techniques to design and drive the workshop and ensure its success.

This focus area is all about listening to the *Chorus of the Customer,* or the many voices of the customer. I will address this more in chapter 9, but the key point is to know who sings the melody and who sings the harmonies. In other words, know who makes the decisions and who influences the person/people who make the decisions.

With the Customer, for the Customer. Consider having a Black Belt working at the customers' premises to be on hand full time to support them and solve their problems. The Black Belt becomes a trusted member of the team and may be given information directly by the customer themselves about their concerns, capability gaps, or other issues that could lead to opportunities for new business. Make sure your customers are aware of the benefits of your brand of Six Sigma so they can use it on a daily basis. Six Sigma becomes a common language.

Increasing Customer Success. Show your customer how Six Sigma can help them succeed. Make your customer shine. Imagine how well your customers will feel about a company that helps get them promoted or awarded a large pay raise. And don't forget to cure your customer's insomnia. Always remember that your customer has a customer, too. Help your customers help their customers be successful. If Six Sigma tools, methods, and techniques work on your processes, they should also work on your customers' processes. In fact, Six Sigma tools, techniques, and methods work on any process.

Partnering through the Value Chain. Form a long-term partnering arrangement with your customer or with your suppliers—better yet, form it with both. Suggest that your version of Six Sigma is the common language throughout the value chain. Work together to solve problems and to visualize the desired future state. Use a Six Sigma workshop to design and develop the governance, vision, goals, and strategy for the partnership.

Customer Engagement. Develop a process to ensure that your customers understand Six Sigma. Use it as a competitive advantage. Brief the customer often on how Six Sigma has helped solve your organization's internal problems, and more importantly, how it can be used to increase your customer's success. Share success stories to generate pull from the customer.

Growth Diagnosis. Hold a facilitated series of workshops to help business leaders and business developers identify, assess, and prioritize growth opportunities. This focus area enables organizations to understand the state of balance between the What, How, and Why of projects to ensure that discretionary investment is being made where it will result in the most impact. The output should be a focused direction and agreement on where to align company investments and resources. Use Six Sigma tools to help define the current state, find the undesirable effects (UDEs)[2] of this current state, and then conduct a root-cause analysis to find the real problem and not just the symptom. Once the root cause has been found, you can jointly

---

2   UDEs were introduced by Eliyahu Goldratt, author of *The Goal* and *Critical Chain*

develop solutions. Discretionary funds are always at a premium. New product developments that are balanced have a greater chance of success. New business proposals that are balanced are more likely to succeed. With this information, an organization can make knowledge-based decisions.

Defining Solutions. Hold facilitated workshops to help understand and define solutions that meet customer needs. These workshops are usually internal and look at developing solutions with the customer for the opportunities identified. The Quality Function Deployment (QFD) tool works great here, especially if the customer helps you validate the QFD results. The QFD transforms customer needs into engineering or other characteristics of a product or service. The QFD helps the organization to prioritize on the critical characteristics of a new product or service from the viewpoint of the customer.

This focus area can really help enable the success of new product developments by ensuring that the balance between the What, How, and Why is addressing the needs of the macro and micro marketplace and customers. In other words, it focuses on both the changing trends of the macro environment and the specific needs of customers.

Increasing the Probability of Capture (P Capture). Organize a series of activities to optimize the probability of winning new business, beginning as early as possible in the capture process. The capture process takes an organization from an initial idea to the final winning proposal. This focus area enables more efficient proposal preparation, leading to offers the customer actually needs and wants. A proposal that is balanced has a much higher chance of success than one that is unbalanced. Six Sigma tools and methods can help create winning strategies that are balanced and compelling. The outcome on the competitive proposals I have studied is a higher ratio of wins.

Six Sigma professionals have an arsenal of tools at their disposal. The table in figure 3.3 provides an example of tools that can be applied in each of the focus areas. See Appendix A for a brief description of each of these tools.

Focus Area	Tools
Identifying Customer Needs	Listening, VOC, QFD, Brainstorming, Affinitization, Decision Tree, 5-Whys
With the Customer, for the Customer	Tools dictated by the situation
Increasing Customer Success	Tools dictated by the situation
Partnering through the Value Chain	Tools dictated by the situation
Customer Engagement	Tools dictated by the situation
Growth Diagnosis	Process Maps, Critical Chain, Brainstorming, Root-Cause Analysis, 5-Whys, Affinitization
Defining Solutions	QFD, FMEA, Visioning, Brainstorming, TRIZ
Increasing P Capture	Critical Chain, Workshops, QFD, FMEA, Brainstorming, TRIZ

Figure 3.3. Six Sigma Growth Tools

Often, the Six Sigma focus areas complement one another as the business opportunity evolves. The diagram on the next page shows an example of how the areas may work together in a process flow.

In the flow example, the output from one focus area activity—for example, a Growth Diagnosis—will form part of the input to one of the other focus areas—for example, Solution Definition or Partnering. The point is that Six Sigma tools and methods can enable the successful pursuit of business opportunities from the initial customer need through order receipt. The beauty is that Six Sigma can work in high-tech manufacturing companies, financial institutions, restaurants, education, governments, and even entertainment. In other words, Six Sigma and the focus areas can enable success for any organization.

Perhaps these focus areas will work in your organization. At least they should provide food for thought. Create your own focus areas,

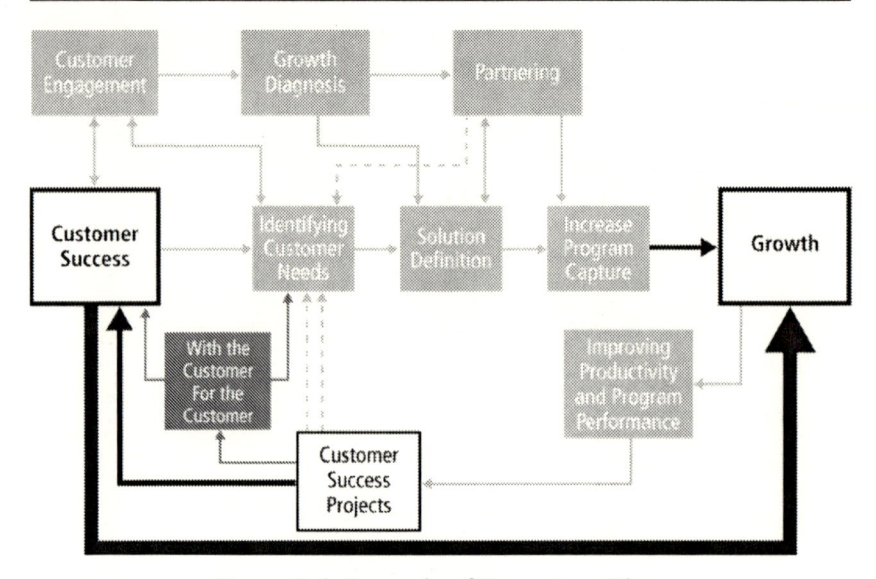

Figure 3.4. Example of Focus Area Flow

use the eight I suggest (they work!) or modify them based on your own experience and needs. You may not need eight focus areas. Pick one or two that will help ignite your efforts to achieving out-of-this-world levels of success.

Profitable business growth is more important than ever, yet markets are more competitive and profits are being squeezed. Organizations are looking for new ways to deal with this paradox, which is exactly why we must be more innovative. These challenges are very much externally focused, and Six Sigma needs to be externally focused as well. Hence, there is a pressing need for Six Sigma at the front end of business to address Innovation for Growth.

The principles of Six Sigma and its tools and methods are universal. Please consider your Six Sigma Black Belts as strategic partners. Have the Black Belts' annual goals match those of the vice president. If it is all about focusing on the customer, your Six Sigma Black Belts can help provide that focus.

Six Sigma provides processes and standards, not just "program of the month" initiatives.

Six Sigma is about defining the current state, visualizing the desired future state, and providing the tools and techniques to help you get there. In the golden age of the Greek Empire, when great philosophers like Socrates and Aristotle were helping change the way we think, "Gnothe Seauton" was engraved in large letters over the entrance to the Athenian Temple.[3] The words, which mean "know thyself," were considered essential knowledge by the wise of the time. Innovation and Six Sigma start from the position of knowing thyself from an intellectual, human, and organizational viewpoint. If you don't know thyself (i.e., understand the current state) it is impossible to fix the problem and/or create the future.

Take Six Sigma to your customers in a helpful way, and you will see them change from dissatisfied to satisfied, and eventually become delighted. In short, make your customers successful. And remember, even your customers have customers. How can you collectively make the end user successful?

Be passionate about your customers, and use Six Sigma to help them succeed. Choose a diverse and enthusiastic team to drive it forward, and get the support of the high-paid help (CEO and team). Use Six Sigma tools and methods to drive Innovation because Innovation drives Growth. Be sure to focus your Innovations on your customers' needs. Six Sigma is ready to be taken to the next level of Innovation, growth, and customer success. Use it to help set strategies and tactics to achieve your goals, and watch your business grow.

3   Joseph J. Weed, *Wisdom of the Mystic Masters*

Key Points in Chapter 3

- » Strategic use of Six Sigma is about focusing on the big picture.
- » Six Sigma can and should be used to enable Innovation and Growth.
- » Use Six Sigma to help bridge the Innovation Gap.
- » Both Innovation and Six Sigma define the current state, visualize the desired future state, and provide techniques to help to get you there.
- » Six Sigma enables Innovation by pulling together the ideas, energy, and passions of the intellectual, organizational, and human factors.
- » Have a balanced approach to Innovation; use Six Sigma to help you get that balance.
- » Partner Six Sigma Black Belts with business leaders.
- » Partner Six Sigma Black Belts with your customers.
- » Create common language, behaviors, and culture through Six Sigma with your customers, partners, and suppliers.
- » Challenge Six Sigma to solve the big problems.
- » Focus on the business goals, not specific Six Sigma goals.

Key Questions to Ask Yourself

- » Do you have a Six Sigma program? If not, why not?
- » Is your Six Sigma program strategically focused or immersed in tactics?
- » Is your Six Sigma program internally focused, externally curious, or both?
- » How do you attack the big issues that face your organization?
- » Is your Six Sigma program focused on the success of your customers?
- » How can you start a Six Sigma program today to enable Innovation and create the future you desire?

chapter 4

six sigma in a smaller business

There are essentially two types of organizations that Six Sigma can help: those that have a Six Sigma program but need to take it to the next level because it has become stagnant or stale, and those that for one reason or another have not yet introduced Six Sigma. The former may have found their Six Sigma programs to have stagnated or lost support; the latter are probably not yet convinced of the value. There is also a third type of organization that doesn't use Six Sigma: the successful market leader that addresses issues and problems in other ways. This type of organization may use many of the tools and principles of Six Sigma without having a formal Six Sigma program. These organizations do have some form of strategy for continuous improvement and Innovation.

The largest group of organizations who haven't yet introduced Six Sigma are smaller businesses. How you define "smaller business" depends on your perspective. According to the New Business Association of America,[1] the U.S. government defines small businesses in heavy engineering and construction as those that earn less than $31 million per year. In agriculture, the figure is $750,000 per year, and travel agencies are considered to be small businesses if their annual revenue is less than $3.1 million. The business could be a startup, or it could be established. It could be in manufacturing or retail, or it could be a service provider. Whatever the size and nature of the smaller business, there is a Six Sigma program that will benefit it.

---

1   www.sba.gov, 2007

Why Six Sigma?

Why should a smaller business want to embark on a continuous improvement program such as Six Sigma? What level of investment would it take? How long before there is a positive return on investment? What kind of training would be required? How do they start?

Smaller business leaders often pose these and other questions. They have every resource working as hard as possible, every dollar being used, and every second of every day bringing a hive of activity. *If only there was more time to strategize and innovate. If only we could find a few more customers. If only we could be more efficient. If only we didn't have as many defects. If only our days didn't seem like endless firefighting! If only ...*

Now, with Six Sigma, smaller businesses can introduce what has until now been a luxury enjoyed almost exclusively by larger organizations.

It is true that smaller businesses rarely have more time or money than their leaders know what to do with. But it is also true that smaller businesses have ambitions: to grow, to yield greater profits, and to have delighted and loyal customers. And many smaller businesses have the potential to be great innovators. A small business is usually run by entrepreneurs, and entrepreneurs are driven by the need to make a difference and achieve success. Smaller organizations can actually benefit more than their larger counterparts by taking advantage of the link between Six Sigma, Innovation, and Growth. Entrepreneurs usually know the What and the Why; it is the How they often need help with, and Six Sigma has proven to be a key methodology in achieving the How. Six Sigma can help entrepreneurs achieve the What, How, Why Balance.

A Six Sigma program in a smaller business doesn't have to start company-wide, it doesn't need heavy investment, and it doesn't need to involve weeks of training that takes key personnel away from day-to-day jobs.

Six Sigma in a smaller business is more about principles, behaviors, and culture. It is about developing good habits and always working toward providing value to the customer. Six Sigma is about characterizing the current state, having a vision about the desired future state, and charting a path to get there. It is about ensuring that the intellectual, organizational, and human factors are balanced.

In figure 4.1, the current state, depicted by the isolated island, is hardly desirable. A beautiful tropical beach represents the desired future state. A major constraint could be the strength of the wind. *If only we had a stronger wind at our backs!* The sharks represent a barrier to success, which here are being ridden by your competitors. *Why are our competitors trying to eat us alive?* One path to chart could be to bypass the competition and travel where there are fewer, or better yet, no sharks. To overcome the constraint, you might include a motor on the rowing boat, a bigger set of oars, or a sail. Maybe there is an opportunity to get a better boat. No matter how difficult it may seem to get to the desired future state, there is always a way, and Six Sigma is an excellent methodology to enable you to find the way and then get you there.

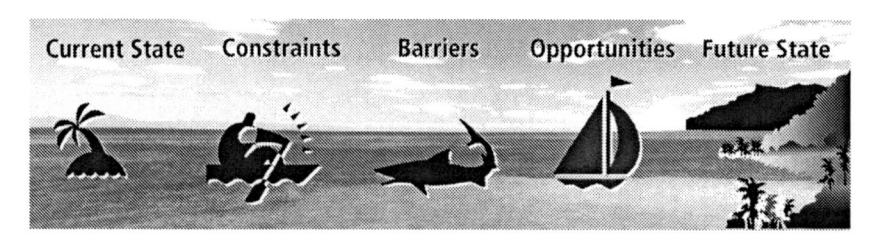

Figure 4.1. Charting a Path to the Desired State

Because there is no one-size-fits-all Six Sigma program, smaller businesses can reap the benefits by initiating a Six Sigma program that is appropriate. In chapter 2, I introduced the DMAIC methodology as being the most widely used system adopted by companies using Six Sigma. Many variations exist, such as DMADV (Define, Measure, Analyze, Design, Verify) and DMEDI (Design, Measure, Explore, Develop, Implement). My own experience with Raytheon Six Sigma used a six-step method known as the wheel. In the following chapter, you will learn about the 5-D methodology, which can be very effective in developing opportunities. Unlike the traditional Six Sigma methods, the 5-D method relies less on analysis and root cause, allowing the user to quickly turn the idea into reality.

A smaller company can use one of these or another method. It could also simply bring Six Sigma into its own existing continuous improvement process, assuming it has one. It is all about getting from the undesired current state to the desired future state.

Getting Started

It will be prudent to start small, with one or two projects. See the benefit of these projects and reinvest the savings or some of the increased revenue. You could start by fixing a problem in a process, reducing waste, or driving variation out of a process. You could start with an Innovation or Growth workshop (see chapter 17). Wherever you start, you should not only address what is important, but also what is urgent. Urgency is a great way to get the attention of business leaders. You could start with a workshop or Kaizen[2] event that will identify some actions or projects.

Prioritizing your projects when you start is vital. Don't take on too many projects at once, and don't take on projects that are too big (i.e., those that will take months and months to complete). These common failure modes are akin to trying to boil the ocean and solving world hunger. Go for the low-hanging fruit—the projects that will produce early benefits that the organization can easily see and appreciate. However, it is equally important not to fabricate projects that should really be solved by common sense; the organization will see right through that. For example, it would be a waste of effort and resource to use Six Sigma to decide how to refurnish a conference room. When prioritizing your projects, try applying the RAM rule: is the project relevant, achievable, and manageable? Make sure the results will have a direct benefit to the customer. An effective Six Sigma project will exhibit the right What, How, Why Balance.

What will a startup project look like? It will more than likely be centered in the project owners' workplace and be sponsored by a member of the leadership team. It will lead to some form of measur-

---

2   Japanese word meaning "continuous improvement"; an event is often a compressed Six Sigma project during which a team moves from Define to Control in a few days

able results and be accomplished in a short period of time, probably less than two months. A startup project will either reduce costs, reduce cycle time, lower risk, improve quality, or improve performance in some other way, such as enabling growth or Innovation. A good startup project will help you improve the way you do your job, and it will be relevant, achievable, and manageable.

You will need some basic training, but try to make sure you select a program that is focused on smaller businesses, rather than a corporate-style program that has been made available through a series of public offerings. A four-hour training program will be enough to get you started. When you start to see the benefits, you will be hooked and will want to seek out more engagements and more training.

You shouldn't need a sophisticated tool kit to start your Six Sigma journey. Even Black Belts tend to use only a few tools for almost all situations. You shouldn't need detailed statistics experts to blind you with science and jargon. You can develop your tools and statistics expertise when your Six Sigma program is established, if you feel it is necessary and can justify the benefits. This may ensure that you keep your initial projects relevant, achievable, and manageable.

Some simple tools you could start with include creative brainstorming, 5-Whys,[3] and COMMWIP (seven types of waste: Correction, Overproduction, Movement of Material or Information, Motion of Employees, Waiting or Wasting Time, Inventory, and Processing). The best tool to use in every case is the simplest, easiest tool that will help you get the job done. Other tools and methods, such as a Growth-shop or a Growth Diagnosis, can help to focus the mind and efforts toward Innovation and growth (see chapter 17).

If you are about to hire new employees, you could consider hiring a ready-made Black Belt or Green Belt. The advantage is that you would have a new resource that is already trained in Six Sigma tools and techniques; the downside is that the person won't know the culture of your organization and won't have a social network yet within the company (but neither will any new hire).

---

3   Method for finding the root cause of a problem by continually asking why until there is no further explanation

Gaining Momentum

You will need a champion on the leadership team, and that champion, depending on the size of the organization, may be the owner or CEO. You will need to communicate your intentions in a clear and concise way. No good will come from an organization with a strategy and champion if you don't get buy-in from key stakeholders. And please try to avoid using jargon. Jargon will likely alienate the program before it has begun. As part of your communications, use a few examples of successes, which can be found through organizations like iSixSigma or the International Society of Six Sigma Professionals (ISSSP)[4]. Contact the Six Sigma leadership teams of companies like GE, Motorola and Raytheon and ask for advice. It's amazing how useful free advice can be and the Six Sigma leaders can easily be found via the companies web pages.

Communicate often to show how results are changing the fortune of the company and delighting your customers. You could also start a network with your classmates from the training class to share best practices and answer each other's questions.

When Six Sigma is implemented strategically, it can be the glue that holds the organization together, it can help reduce and eliminate waste and variation, and it can contribute to both top-and bottom-line growth. It can also be used to enable Innovation by helping leaders and managers to make knowledge-based decisions on new product development investment. A successful Six Sigma deployment will transform the relationship between customers, employees, and suppliers. Six Sigma is not rigid; it is not a set of rules that cannot be broken. It is agile and flexible. Six Sigma is a recipe that enables companies to continually exceed customer and shareholder expectations.

[4] www.isssp.com

Key Points in Chapter 4

- » The What, How, Why Balance is key to the success of a smaller business.
- » Six Sigma can reinvigorate your continuous improvement program.
- » Six Sigma can enable the ambitions of smaller businesses.
- » Host a Growth-shop or Innovation workshop.
- » Prioritize your projects by using the RAM rule.
- » All business have ambitions and challenges; many don't have the time or skills to work on them.
- » Six Sigma in a smaller business is about principles, behaviors, culture, and habits—all focused on the success of the customer.
- » The Six Sigma methodology can chart the path to the desired future state.
- » Start small to prove the benefits.
- » Take an appropriate training class.
- » A basic Six Sigma tool kit can help reap tremendous rewards.
- » Have a passionate Six Sigma champion lead the program.
- » Get advice from some of the leading Six Sigma companies.
- » Communicate early and often.

Key Questions to Ask Yourself

- » How balanced are your intellectual, organizational, and human factors?
- » How do you make the time to improve and grow your business?
- » How would a Six Sigma program help your organization?
- » Can you describe why balance is key to your personal success?
- » Can you describe how balance is key to the success of your organization?
- » Do you know where and how to get Six Sigma training?
- » What areas in your business need improving?

» How do you plan to grow your business?
» How can you be more creative to fuel Innovation?
» Are you on the threshold of something big but just can't find the time to get you there? What can you do about it?

chapter 5

5-D project success

Turning an idea into reality is a rare occurrence. I can't remember how many cool thoughts I've had in the past, talked to a few people who said "wow," and then did nothing about it. Indeed I usually forget about the idea until a few years down the road and there it is, my great idea, made available by somebody else and making that somebody else a gazillion dollars. "Not fair!" I cry, but of course it's fair; it was my fault for not doing something with the dream. So now I follow the 5-D methodology (see figure 5.1). Simply put, the 5-D methodology is Dream It, Design It, Develop It, Deliver It, and Drive It. 5-D is an uncomplicated way to put discipline into any task. The 5-D methodology is Six Sigma for Innovation and Growth, and it truly bridges the Innovation Gap, or the gap between the two hemispheres of the brain. If DMAIC has been widely accepted as the industry standard for traditional Six Sigma, then the 5-D methodology can become the standard for Six Sigma for Innovation and Growth.

Let's look at the methodology in more detail.

Dream It. Everything starts with a vision, a nucleus of an idea. Recently I had the idea to redesign a training course I was responsible for teaching. The course was full of amazing information about using Six Sigma to enable business growth. Unfortunately, it was delivered in a death-by-PowerPoint® way that soon left my students gasping for air. My dream was to make the learning more experiential by introducing a story to the class. The story starts in the days before a fictitious company, BlueSky Aerospace, has developed a growth strategy. In fact, their customers don't have much of a strategy either. BlueSky, with the help of Six Sigma Black Belts, conducts a series

5-D Process

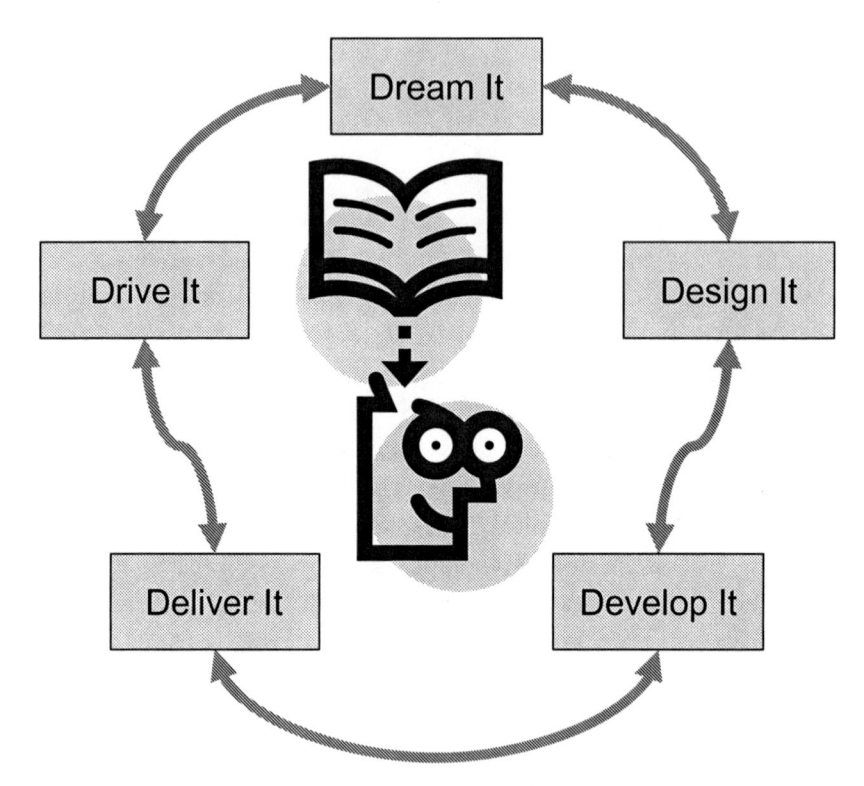

Figure 5.1. The 5-D Methodology

of workshops with the customer and helps create a new operational requirement that becomes a major competitive opportunity.

The class, with the aid of thirteen experiential BlueSky case studies, moves from the initial gleam in the customer's eye, through capture planning and win strategy-development, into a competition for a major business opportunity. The students develop their own story as they move from case to case. They are able to use the story they develop in conjunction with some carefully crafted scenarios as they move through the various phases of the capture process. My dream to make the learning an experience had passion, but it was still just a dream. We were in the right hemisphere of creativity. We still needed to bridge the Innovation Gap and bring the idea to reality. We were ready to start the design of the material.

Design It. The design phase started with a template, an idea as to how the story would develop. I introduced a few measles (situations designed to throw the students off course by changing the environment that forces changes in strategy). We also identified a list of characters to make it real. I also wanted to reuse as much of the existing material as I could; there was no point in reinventing the wheel. The class was designed to be a mix of classroom and experiential learning—full immersion. Stephen R. Covey in his book *The 8th Habit: From Effectiveness to Greatness*, recently added to the old saying that a picture is worth a thousand words by saying that an experience is worth a thousand pictures. The design of the class addressed the need for this type of experience. The students would attend a short module in class, and then go try the learning against the next phase of the case study. Finally, after the crescendo of a competition between two halves of the same class of students, we would hold a reflection period and prepare an action plan about how they would take the learning back to the workplace. When the design was complete we knew what we needed to do, and we knew where the major challenges were. We were still in the right hemisphere of the brain, but now we were ready to bridge the gap.

Develop It. Bringing the course to life was the next stage in the 5-D process—the development stage. To develop such a complex course, I needed help. I recruited a number of subject matter experts (SMEs) from win strategy and proposal backgrounds to bring the little details that are so necessary to ensure success. I also recruited a couple of colleagues that I knew were good storytellers to help bring some of the characters to life. When we had the course materials complete, the case studies written, and an idea on prerequisites, it was time to throw ourselves to the lions and test what we had created. I invited an esteemed group of different SMEs to a red team review. A *red team review* is where they considered the objectives for the learning experience and assessed how well the course would meet those objectives. Reviews are essential in development, and this was no exception. We burned the midnight oil to implement the changes that the red team review identified. We went to print, and in February 2006, we were ready for the first class. The Develop It stage was where we overcame the challenges and bridged the gap.

Deliver It. In this stage you need to consider how the solution, service, or product will be delivered. What will the product, solution, or service be used for? How will the customer use it? Will it be user friendly? Will the logistics team understand the instructions and get it finished on time? Where will it be delivered to? In our case, it was a ballroom at the Dulles Hilton, the location of the inaugural training class. All the instructors arrived, and yours truly led them through a final pep talk. We were ready.

Drive It. Sustainment is the last key part of the 5-D process, otherwise known as Drive It. We had a process for the logisticians, a process for the students to sign up, a process for travel, and a process for the instructor faculty. Knock on wood—the class is a roaring success. Without sustainment, we would have nothing to show but the experience of writing a cool story and creating an interesting training course. By driving it, we were helping professional people develop their skills, potential, and worth. And the evidence is there to see: approximately 50 percent of the Black Belt projects I have seen at certification boards are focused on growth.

The Dream It and Design It phases involve right-brain thinking. The Deliver It and Drive It phases involve left-brain thinking, and the Develop It phase bridges the gap by turning the idea into reality and overcoming the challenges.

The 5-D process works as illustrated by this brief example, but it also works for products, services, and other solutions. Bring in the customer as early as you can, and keep him or her involved throughout the process. The best thing about the 5-D process is its simplicity. You can use it for personal reasons just as easily; for example, you can use the process to help you move, buy a new car, or landscape your garden. It adds some rigor to your intuition.

Some Tools to Support 5-D

Both Six Sigma and Innovation professionals use an abundance of tools. Within the 5-D methodology, you could try using some of the tools shown in figure 5.2. All of these tools are commonly used with the exception of RAM and the Balance Indicator, both explained in Appendix A, along with the other tools referred to in this book.

	Suggested Tools
Dream It	VOC, SWOT, Brainstorming, 5-Whys, Creative Thinking, IPO, Force Field Analysis, Mind Mapping, RAM
Design It	Balance Indicator, QFD, FMEA, Brainstorming, RACI, IPO, Force Field Analysis, Storytelling, VOC, RAM
Develop It	Balance Indicator, QFD, FMEA, RACI, DOE, IPO, Force Field Analysis, Communications Plan, TOC, Storytelling, VOC
Deliver It	Balance Indicator, RACI, IPO, VOC, Storytelling
Drive It	IPO, RACI, VOC
Note	Throughout the project it is recommended that you constantly reassess your balance, get continuous feedback from the customer (VOC), and use a Stage/Gate methodology to ensure that funding is controlled.

Figure 5.2. Suggested Tools

Double-Loop 5-D

Of course, the 5-D methodology best enables Innovation when considering the external environment. Figure 5.3 shows how double-loop learning 5-D ensures that we are focused on the areas that will make a positive difference to our customers and society. The external loop helps us understand where the insertion point may be (i.e., what needs are we addressing?). The Understand It phase is concerned with looking at the macro environment—the market, social, economic and demographic needs—and the Observe It phase looks at the micro environment by viewing real people in real life. Once we understand the macro and micro environments, we have more of a chance of introducing something new that adds value (i.e., Innovation). The Test It phase allows us to make sure that we are providing solutions to the customer's needs. Feedback from the Test It phase allows us to make any necessary changes.

The redesign of the training class was in fact a double-loop 5-D implementation. The team started from an understanding of the external factors. We asked what the business leaders needed to help

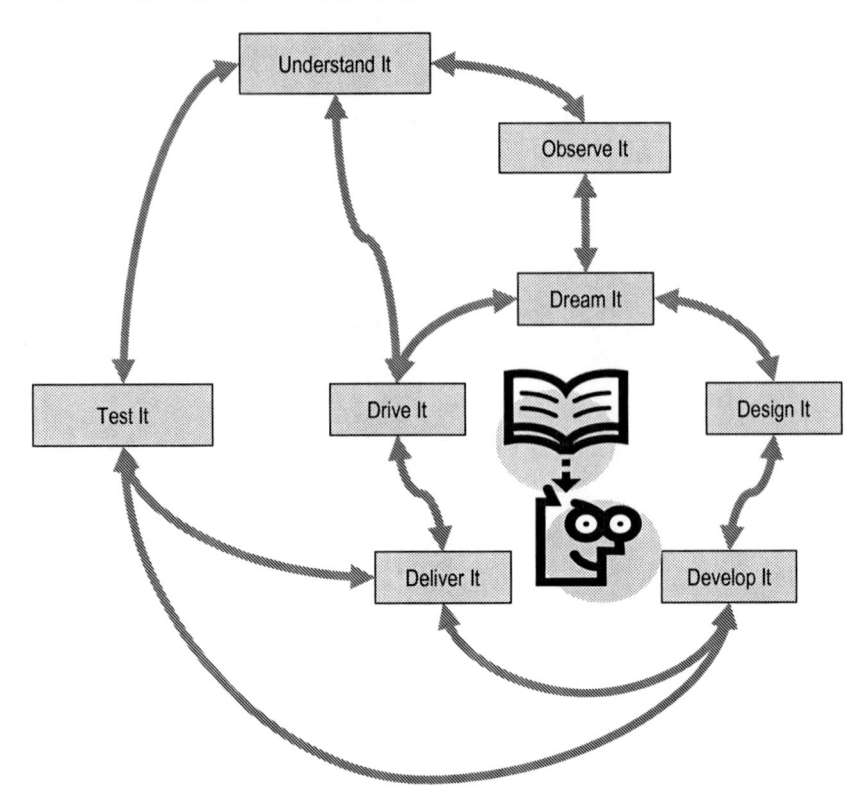

Figure 5.3. Double-Loop 5-D

them grow. We then observed the class during training and observed Black Belts as they worked on growth projects. We studied the certification process and through these actions brought a thorough understanding of the current state to the Dream It phase. When we were ready to go, we tested the material at a peer (red team) review. Since implementation, we have gone back into the market and are currently in the outer loop assessing the next effort. This will likely include a new approach to the way we promote and market the class.

Success

We have previously shown that the right balance between the intellectual, organizational, and human factors is critical to success. We have also suggested that success is driven by passion. So if balance and passion are the keys to success, and the 5-D process can help get you there, what is success?

- » Success is the progressive realization of a worthy goal.[1]
- » Progressive realization is achieved one day at a time.
- » Do your best each day, and that day will be successful.
- » Five consecutive successful days defines a successful week.
- » Four consecutive successful weeks means a successful month.
- » Consecutive successful months lead to a successful life, career, project, and so on.

Create a vision, define the goal(s) required to achieve the vision, ensure that each day is a success, and you will realize the vision—as long as it has the right What, How, Why Balance.

One simple technique I use in conjunction with 5-D is to reflect on where I am at the end of each day. I think of the five or six most important things I need to achieve the following day to stay on target, and I write them down. The next morning I already know the five or six most important things I need to do. Of course I get derailed, just as everybody else does, but I have found that by starting with a simple plan of action, I almost always have a successful day.

The 5-D methodology is really suited to the Creative (conceptual and entertainment) Age. The Dream It and Design It phases start in the right hemisphere of the brain. The Develop It phase transitions from the right hemisphere to the left, thus bridging the Innovation Gap. The Deliver It and Drive It phases are about tactical execution, which is left-brain dominant. By embracing the 5-D methodology to enable strategic projects, we can show that the Creative Age is also the age of Six Sigma for Innovation.

---

1   Earl Nightingale, *Lead the Field*

Key Points in Chapter 5

- » Dream It, Design It, Develop It, Deliver It, and Drive It.
- » Use the 5-D methodology to bridge the Innovation Gap through Six Sigma.
- » The 5-D Method addresses balance, which is designed into the process, developed, and then delivered.
- » Use the 5-D methodology to achieve success.
- » An experience is worth a thousand pictures.
- » Success is the progressive realization of a worthy goal.
- » Double-loop 5-D helps focus our Innovation on adding real value.
- » Plan each day for success.
- » Ensure that your vision and goals address the What, How, Why Balance.

Key Questions to Ask Yourself

- » Why do you have dreams that never turn into reality?
- » How do you plan each day for success?
- » What are you planning to do tomorrow to ensure that it is a successful day?
- » How do you sustain or drive a project once the initial delivery has been made?
- » What projects have you started or are about to start that could benefit from a 5-D approach?

chapter 6

why world-class is not enough

A Rolls Royce and Buggy Whips

When I first started my career, being best in class was enough. The world was a vast place, but most companies were locally focused. You knew your competition and your customers. Shortly thereafter, we embarked on being world-class—in other words, being renowned for producing really great products and services. Being the best in the world at making turbine generators, for example, guaranteed profitable business and high shareholder value. Then the market saturated. When I was a child, everybody wanted a Rolls Royce; now a Rolls Royce is just another BMW.

As an analogy, let's think of a sports team that two years ago celebrated its second straight world championship. Did the competition sit down and accept the situation? No way. Last year's champions become this year's losers. Being best in class or world-class is good, but for only a snapshot in time.

My family, the Carters, were once fairly rich and powerful. The name originates from the cart, which in Medieval England meant that we owned the transportation from the farms to market. As time moved on, we expanded into personal transport with buggies. But we didn't stop with agricultural and personal transport; we joined the industrial age and quickly moved into manufacturing, becoming the world's premier supplier of buggy whips. We totally owned the market. Buggy whips came in lots of styles and types, to fit every taste. Then some fool invented the automobile. How did the Carters respond? We made even better buggy whips—cheaper, faster to market, prettier.

We were still world-class and best in class, but we didn't listen to the market; we continued to do things right, but weren't doing the right things. If only we had understood the importance of balancing the What and How with the Why and started to make parts for the automobile! There are now more automobiles in the United States than there are people with driver's licenses. Imagine having a product on each car that returned just one dollar of profit!

Then there are the slide-rule manufacturers and the typewriter makers. Where are the world-class and best-in-class typewriter producers today? Do you even know what a slide rule is? Look how the music medium has changed over the last few years. We now carry around thousands of songs with us on something the size of a credit card. Organizations often fail to see the need to change because they are successful under current market conditions. This can be their downfall when market conditions are altered and the organization doesn't respond.

The Shrinking World and New Expectations

The world continues to shrink. The economies of China and India are thriving and jobs continue to move to these countries, particularly service-related jobs such as help desks. But these new economies won't stop there. There are ten times more engineers graduating in India and China now than in the United States. We need to continue to stay ahead, to be more creative in thought and more innovative in deed, and to continually thrive to find new markets and new ways of doing things. By releasing these service-related jobs to countries far and wide, we either have a problem—loss of jobs—or an opportunity—available people to help create new value.[1] I prefer to think in terms of the latter. Individuals, groups, and companies that also adopt this viewpoint will be successful. Those that don't will soon see their engineering, design, and development jobs joining the service sector in those faraway places.

We are no longer merely judged against our peers and the competition in our fields; we are judged against everybody. Your customers

---

1   Thomas Friedman, *The World Is Flat*

are also the customers of Disney and Starbucks, of Lexus and the Ritz-Carlton. When your customers witness something extraordinary from your noncompetitors, they start to expect it from everybody they deal with. A luxury once experienced becomes a necessity (just like Lexi and the plasma TV). We judge ourselves by our values, but we judge others by their behaviors. If we were to meet today for the first time, I would have no idea what your values are. However, simply by observing you, I would easily detect and understand your behaviors. I would therefore judge you on those behaviors. We can conclude that we are all judged by our behaviors. And those behaviors are judged against those companies who are providing out-of-this-world service. To move to out-of-this-world levels of performance requires us to constantly evaluate our behaviors and habits, developing patterns that help us consistently improve. Six Sigma and 5-D are ideal methodologies to help us to do this and achieve the What, How, Why Balance that enables success.

Going beyond world-class means not only striving to be the best of the best, but obtaining a long-term, big-picture view as well. It is about executing strategies that ensure you remain the best of the best. It isn't just about separating the forest from the trees; it is about climbing the tallest tree to make sure you are in the right forest! Use Six Sigma tools and methodologies to "know thyself" and develop a thorough understanding of the current state. Use it to drive your strategic visioning, to understand the constraints and barriers to success, to drill down to the root causes, and to help understand where the opportunities are to overcome those barriers and constraints. Creatively using Six Sigma in an innovative way will help you define the solutions needed to drive success. Six Sigma helps you understand the current state of the balance between your intellectual, organizational, and human factors that dictate your strategies and how you approach major new business opportunities.

Remember the diagram shown again in figure 6.1! Six Sigma helps you chart the path to get to the desired future state that is balanced Innovation. The barriers to balance could be that you perceive your technology to be better than everybody else's or that your sales-and-marketing team is the best in the world or that your products are unbeatable. Your constraints could involve your current organization.

Does your organization enable Innovation or get in its way? Does your organization understand the need for the What, How, Why Balance? Do you constantly hear comments like "We've always done it that way"?

Figure 6.1. Charting a Route to the Desired State

I once heard motivational speaker and author of *New Sales Speak*, Terri Sjodin, tell a great story about a missionary in Africa. He sat with a small group of children and proceeded to open a banana. All the children started laughing because he opened the banana from the pointed end where it is attached to the tree. Apparently the correct way is to pinch the flat end; it automatically splits, and you peel it with no strings and no mush. Millions of people in the western world have been doing it wrong just because it was always done that way. (I know you are reaching for a banana right now to try it.) Like nature showed these African children the easy way to open a banana, Six Sigma can show us the easiest way to overcome barriers and constraints. Don't allow the "we've always done it that way" brigade to get in the way of success.

Use Six Sigma to show you the most suitable way. Six Sigma can help develop the most appropriate path to reach the desired future state. It can help bridge the Innovation Gap by turning creative ideas into delivered reality. Six Sigma enables us to achieve the What, How, Why Balance.

Always doing things the same way can be a trap. We should continually challenge our assumptions. Even a company that has a balanced Innovation model today will likely be unbalanced tomorrow, probably due to external factors. Disruptive technologies happen, customers' emotional and rational needs evolve, and social networks change. Why didn't IBM think about the Dell business model? They allowed a new entrant to the PC marketplace because they failed to realize the potential of organizational Innovation. Why didn't Sotheby's invent eBay? Sotheby's had the market to themselves and the emotional connections with customers, but they failed to see the relevance of the intellectual Innovation of the Internet and how it could enable them to expand and grow. The same can be said of Borders and Barnes and Noble. Why didn't one of these world-class companies introduce the world to Amazon? Amazon may have struggled to make a profit at first, but they significantly changed the way many of us purchase our books. All of these companies were successful in their own right but failed to recognize the change in the environment and the opportunities those changes bring. What opportunities are staring at you right now that you can't see? If your current offerings are being made obsolete, make sure that you are the one doing it.

So now that you are ready to look at everything as an opportunity and to look into the mirror to check your behaviors and habits, are you ready to take your organization to the next level?

Key Points in Chapter 6

- » Being best in class and world-class is not enough.
- » The world continues to shrink.
- » A small world presents more opportunity.
- » A luxury once experienced becomes a necessity.
- » We judge ourselves by our values but others by their behaviors.
    - o Use Six Sigma to help define the current state, establish the desired future state, and chart the route to get there.
    - o Don't let the organization get in the way of Innovation.
    - o Use Six Sigma and 5-D to achieve the What, How, Why Balance.

Key Questions to Ask Yourself

- » Do you look at the flattening of the world as an opportunity to thrive? How will you take advantage of this shrinking world? What actions can you and should you take?
- » Do you look in the mirror to study your behaviors? How do you think others perceive your behaviors? Do your behaviors reflect your values? If not, what action are you going to take?
- » Do you have your own buggy whip or slide rule? What is happening in the world to provide an alternative way to fulfill the needs that you currently fill? What can you do about it?
- » Have you used or thought about using Six Sigma to help chart your course to future success?
- » Does your organization get in the way of Innovation through overmanaging or bureaucracy?

chapter 7

unparalyze the paradigm

One of the barriers individuals and organizations face in achieving the What, How, Why Balance is the inability to challenge their existing paradigms.

The definition of a paradigm is "an outstandingly clear or typical example or archetype." As we know from experience, this usually means a very fixed point of view about an issue, based on knowledge and familiarity. Some of our paradigms come from what we learn from people we admire or have worked for. Unfortunately, not all paradigms are positive or relevant, like the Carter paradigm about buggy whips. Paradigms are usually very intransigent. At one time the Swiss were renowned as the greatest watchmakers in the world. They were both world-class and best in class. The digital watch was invented in Switzerland, but the watchmakers were fixed in their paradigms about the beauty and artistry required to make watches. They ignored the new technology until the Japanese company Seiko produced the first mass-available quartz watches.

A paralyzed paradigm will increase the width of the Innovation Gap. It will also strangle Innovation.

Vital Lies

In my experience, many things have caused paradigms to become paralyzed. Two of the most common are *vital lies* and *limiting assumptions*. What is a vital lie? Vital lies offer excuses for not changing. They can prevent the pursuit of the possible. An example of a vital lie might be "we know what our customers want"—when what we really mean is that we know what we want them to have (like the Swiss watchmakers). Another vital lie might be "it's always been done that way"—meaning it doesn't matter if it is good or bad, I'm not going to change. Or perhaps "the automobile industry will never take off"—meaning I'm going to continue to make buggy whips and people will continue to buy them. There are hundreds of different vital lies, such as "the boss will never agree" or "we don't have the budget." Another shocker: "everybody else does it that way." (Did you try peeling the banana yet?) A vital lie is a type of self-deception; it is a way of justifying to yourself that you have no choice.

Vital lies need to be out in the open, recognized early for what they are, and then kicked out. Strategic use of Six Sigma is focused on the external environment, helping provide the evidence to ensure that vital lies are recognized. Six Sigma helps eradicate vital lies by providing the data for knowledge-based solutions. A decision based on knowledge and recognition of the What, How, Why Balance has a much higher chance of leading to success.

Limiting Assumptions

What about limiting assumptions? A limiting assumption is usually stated by a recognized authority on a subject, somebody who has the tacit knowledge and experience to give them an air of superiority on the given subject. Where would we be if these so-called experts were always listened to as if they were preaching the gospel? In his book, *Slay the Dragons Free the Genie*, Bennett A. Neiman provides many great quotes on limiting assumptions. The following are a few of my favorites. Thomas J. Watson, chairman of IBM during the 1940s, confidently said "there is a world market for about five computers"; In 1899, Charles Duell, then-commissioner of the U.S. Patent Office, proudly told the world, "everything that can be invented has already been invented." Famous movie pioneer Darryl F. Zanuck, scoffed in the 1940s, "Video won't be able to hold any market. People will soon get tired of looking at a plywood box every night." I wonder what he would make of plasma TVs and DVD players, not to mention TiVo and pay-per-view. Another favorite is the famous *Business Week* article published in 1968 that boasted "because there are over fifty foreign cars on sale in the USA, the Japanese auto industry isn't likely to carve out a very big slice of the market." Limiting assumptions forced the Carters out of business when the automobile was invented.

Use Six Sigma brainstorming techniques and other tools and methods to help discover the realms of the possible, to understand where the barriers are that will stop you from getting there, and to put in place the action plan to get over those barriers. To paraphrase Walt Disney, if you can dream it, you can achieve it.

To take advantage of the balance between the What, How, and Why, we need to kick out the vital lies when we hear them and challenge the limiting assumptions.

That Confounded Box

Another strange phenomenon that has recently evolved is thinking outside the box. It seems that to be creative you have to think outside the box—in other words, outside the space where you are comfortable. But this is limiting in itself. For example, a new design of a high-tech widget may require a team to be highly creative and think outside of their normal areas, or think outside the box. But this usually facilitates people jumping into another box.

And what happens when the highly creative design folks hand the project over to the development team to turn the dream into reality? (Hopefully the transition will include a few of the designers as well.) Do the developers now have to stay inside the new box? What about being creative inside the box as well? Inside-the-box thinking needs other types of creativity, like creatively finding ways to fund the project or creatively finding resources. Could this be out-of-the-box thinking? Now I don't know whether I'm inside or outside of the box.

I understand that there may be rules to follow when developing the widget, but that doesn't mean creativity has to go. People are usually happy within their realm (i.e., inside the box). This is the comfort zone. But what about those few individuals who seem to be capable of thinking both inside and outside the box? Are these people really unique, or is it a matter of perspective and techniques? Is this Innovation? Is it the transition of ideas from the right brain to the left brain, or from outside to inside the box? I would ask you to consider this simple challenge: what box? By eliminating the box completely, we don't have to worry about thinking inside and outside of it.

There is a story about Disney Imagineers, the folks who design and develop the company's theme parks, rides, and special events. The story goes: Question, "How many Imagineers does it take to screw in a light bulb?" The answer, "Why does it have to be a light bulb?" Get it? What box?

The Evil of "No Because"

I must mention one additional thing here: we must try to eradicate the phrase "no because" from our business vocabulary. Some smart people derive great pleasure from saying "no because." It makes them feel good to be able to kill an idea because they have more information than you do. "No because" is a copout, a vital lie, or an excuse for not taking action. These subject matter experts (SMEs) need to learn how to say "yes if," or better yet "yes and!" This not only affirms an idea but also builds on it. Here's some good advice: develop behaviors where you leave your ego at the door when you enter a meeting room, and stop saying no. If you hear others say "no, because ..." then do as motivational speaker Les Brown suggests and 'make no your vitamin'. In other words, let the word "no" serve as your motivator. Every time you hear a no means you are getting closer to a yes.

Unparalyze your paradigms by recognizing and eradicating vital lies, by challenging limiting assumptions, and by bursting through and eliminating that infuriating box. And stop saying "no because!"

Passion

One final word on the subject of paradigms is about passion. *Passion* is a word I have already used several times in this book. To paraphrase what German philosopher Georg Wilhelm Friedrich Hegel said during his lectures on the *Philosophy of History*, 'nothing was ever achieved without passion'—and this includes breaking paradigms. Passion is the most important aspect of success. Without it, everything you do becomes a chore. If you have little passion for a project, the existence of the box is irrelevant. Passion has many definitions. Following are two of the most relevant to business success: 1) a strong liking, desire, or devotion to some activity, object, or concept and 2) an intense driving feeling or conviction. Passion is about enthusiasm, fervor, and zeal. It is incredibly powerful. Passion is what makes ordinary people like you and me achieve great things. Passion is the first step toward achievement.

I had a highly successful career throughout the 1980s and 1990s in both program management and business development. I used to believe that I was motivated by the hunt, the challenge of competition, and the desire to be successful and admired by peers. However, the key driver was all about helping make my customers successful. Recently, I discovered that my real passion is about helping people succeed in general. Making strong, positive emotional connections with people is what really motivates me. In 2004, I was asked by the vice president of Six Sigma to share my knowledge and experience in an effort to create and deliver a training program in business growth and Six Sigma. I was also to coach and mentor the students as they moved their careers forward. As I mentioned in chapter 5, my dream was to create an experiential learning experience for the students—one that was based as much on making positive emotional connections with faculty and students as it was on information. I encourage the students to share real-life stories because these anecdotes add so many flavors to the learning experience. As Pocahontas sings in the Disney movie, it helps us "sing with all the voices of the mountain and paint with all the colors of the wind."[1] Do your projects and new business proposals sing with all the colors of the wind?

Recognizing the importance of emotional connections really fuelled my passion for helping people succeed; it has created a new career path for me and also inspired me to write this book. My What, How, Why Balance has changed with increased knowledge, and so can yours! Don't resist it; embrace it. Following your passions wisely can have rich rewards. If you are not passionate about your career or the organization that you work for, you might want to consider a change. Each time my balance changes, it coincides with an increase

---

1 Lyrics to the Oscar winning Disney song *Colors of the Wind*, written by Stephen Schwartz, taken from the movie *Pocahontas*

in wisdom. As Solomon suggests in the book of Proverbs, wisdom is more valuable than rubies and gold. Those who pursue wisdom will have success.

Be passionate about what you do and you can unparalyze your paradigms; create the right What, How, Why Balance; and really start to make a positive difference.

Key Points in Chapter 7

- » Paradigms can be moved.
- » Vital lies need to be recognized and eradicated.
- » Limiting assumptions must be challenged.
- » Six Sigma can help us get past vital lies and limiting assumptions by turning data into information.
- » Paradigms stifle Innovation.
- » What box?
- » Eradicate the tyranny of "no because."
- » The What, How, Why Balance can change with new information and knowledge.
- » Passion is one of the keys to success.
- » Make sure your proposals "paint with all the colors of the wind."
- » Pursue wisdom for it is more valuable than gold.

Key Questions to Ask Yourself

- » Do you get anchored to a paradigm? How can you free yourself?
- » How often do you use a vital lie to rationalize a situation? What can you do to eradicate this?
- » Are you accused of thinking too much inside the box or too much outside the box? How can you exterminate the box?
- » Are you passionate about what you do? Do you really believe in it? How can you add more passion to your daily routine? How can you make life fun?
- » If you view your life as a chore, why don't you change its direction? What alternatives are open to you?
- » Can you recognize "no because" for what it is and turn it into a positive "yes if" or "yes and"?

chapter 8

what is growth, anyway?

Where Growth Occurs

To be successful we have to grow. This is true in our personal lives as well as in business. Personal growth is about self-improvement—furthering our education and increasing our knowledge and experience. It is about increasing our wisdom and going into the unknown just because it is there. Personal growth allows us to succeed when we meet new challenges.

Business growth is similar; it is about being successful when we go into the unknown. Growth, like Innovation, is dependent on the What, How, Why Balance. It is also dependent on passion. I've heard many motivational speakers say that we don't fail because we aim too high and miss; we fail because we aim too low and hit. This phrase is attributed to Renaissance artist Michelangelo, and it is easy to see why he was a great success; he had vision, wisdom, and passion.

Business growth can happen both above and below the line, in essentially four areas. Let's consider the growth quadrant in figure 8.1 (next page), which is similar to the Ansoff Matrix[1] so familiar to MBA students.

Most established companies will focus their efforts on the bread and butter of a company's revenue: the comfort zone of existing products with existing customers. That's why the Carters focused

---

1 Igor Ansoff (1918–July 14, 2002) was an applied mathematician and business manager. He is known as the father of Strategic management.

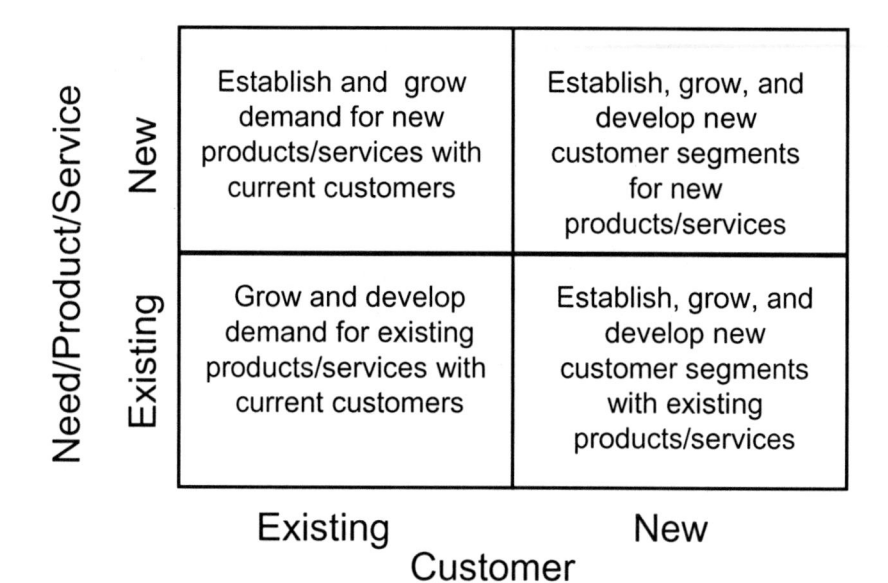

		Existing Customer	New Customer
Need/Product/Service	**New**	Establish and grow demand for new products/services with current customers	Establish, grow, and develop new customer segments for new products/services
	Existing	Grow and develop demand for existing products/services with current customers	Establish, grow, and develop new customer segments with existing products/services

Figure 8.1. The Growth Matrix: Where Growth Happens

their attention on buggy whips. It is also the environment where traditional salespeople work best. They know the customer well, and they get their commission based on the sales they make. Organizations that live in this area are aiming too low and hitting. This comfort zone feels good, but it is insular and can be dangerous because we are ignoring the world around us. The comfort zone is often inside that infuriating box. Our challenge in this new world is to jump into the effective zone. We must find growth in the other three quadrants of the growth matrix. To be successful in the other quadrants, we must balance the intellectual, organizational, and human factors.

So let us consider the upper left quadrant, where we work with our existing customers to try to understand what new products we can sell to them. Traditional sales techniques often do not work in this important realm. One major problem is that we all too often develop the product or service first, and then go to our existing customers and try to sell it to them. A better approach is to listen actively to our customers, and then develop products and services around solutions that fit the customers' future needs. The key word here is *listen*! In order to listen, we need to become anthropologists and ethnographers. Go and see what the customers are struggling with. Establish a relationship where you are the listener. Ask what is bothering them. Findized out what keeps them up at night, and work to develop solutions to their insomnia. This is the Identifying Customer Needs and Increasing Customer Success focus areas that we looked at in chapter 3

Remember the double-loop learning diagram we discussed in chapter 3 and chapter 5? It is shown again in figure 8.2.

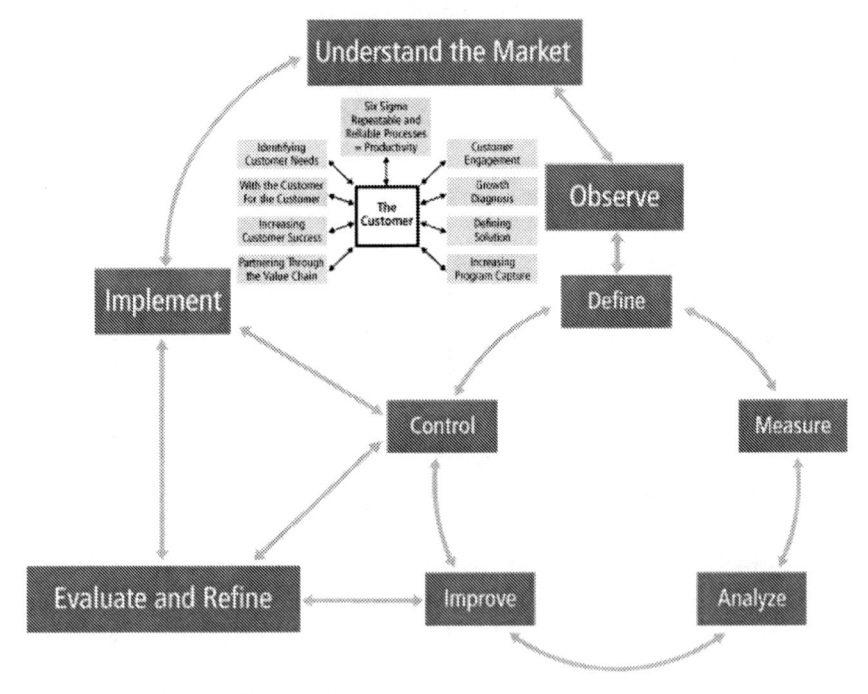

Figure 8.2. Double-Loop Learning with Focus Areas

The outer loop is where we discover opportunities that will help us grow our business. I've added the eight focus areas for Six Sigma to show how we might discover these opportunities and better understand the market.

Moving now to the bottom right quadrant of the growth matrix (figure 8.1), we try to find new customers for our existing products and services. For example, we could try moving into the international marketplace or try making the product more readily available through a different pricing structure or new service offerings. It is also where we might find new ways of combining offerings. The top left quadrant is what Seth Godin generally refers to as the Purple Cow, and the bottom right quadrant is what W. Chan Kim and Renée Mauborgne might describe as the Blue Ocean. Cirque du Soleil found a Purple Cow swimming in the Blue Ocean and hit the top right quadrant with a splash. It is a new business model and offering, addressing a completely new market. Cirque du Soleil isn't a circus or a rock concert or a ballet or the theatre; it is all of these things. Cirque du Soleil provides the audience with something that doesn't exist anywhere else.

The Importance of Balance

To really grow your business requires moving into the top right quadrant, just as Cirque du Soleil did. This is the most difficult area in the growth matrix, and I like to describe it as a green elephant, flying beyond the blue sky and into the stratosphere. This is where Sony was when they developed the Walkman by combining movement, such as jogging, with entertainment. This is where Starbucks was when they discovered that creating an atmosphere for nondrinkers to mix and mingle drew people in to spend money on coffee, which may be a passion of the Starbuck's senior leadership team but is incidental to the experience for most of their customers. It is where Daimler-Benz was when they replaced the buggy with the Mercedes automobile and where Ford was when he made the new, reliable Model T available to anyone.

The Six Sigma focus areas applied through double-loop learning can help us discover opportunities and create strategies that will help us move into all four quadrants of the growth matrix. Your Six Sigma projects and efforts can provide the key to success in these areas.

In chapter 1, we talked about unbalanced Innovation and how it might affect growth. Figure 8.3 shows that unbalanced Innovation is likely to keep us firmly entrenched in the bottom left quadrant. We need to organize ourselves in a way to enable growth. We also need to make positive emotional connections with our customers to create mutual trust and ensure that we completely empathize with them to understand their needs.

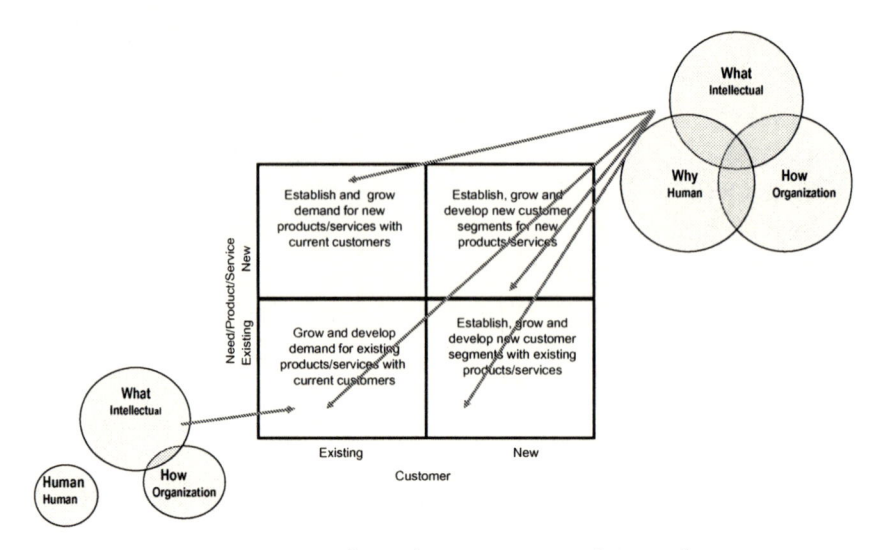

Figure 8.3. Balanced Innovation and Growth

You may have the best technology in the world, but if you can't connect with the customer, you can't tell your story in an innovative and compelling way, or you aren't organized in a way that makes it easy for your customer to do business with you, you are unlikely to grow in adjacent markets. In other words, if you don't have the What, How, Why Balance, you are unlikely to grow with any consistency.

In *Blue Ocean Strategy,* authors W. Chan Kim and Renée Mauborgne introduce the concept of a strategy map to show the distinction between the offering of a company, compared to the industry norm. The book includes many great examples, including: Cirque du Soleil as mentioned above, and Southwest Airlines.

Southwest Airlines focuses on speed. They realized that each minute their aircraft is on the ground is costing them revenue. Their turnaround times have been the fastest in the industry for years. They also introduced point-to-point travel rather than the traditional airline hub-and-spoke methods. Southwest flies routes from one airport to another, similar to how a bus travels from one stop to the next. This means that if an airport is closed, perhaps because of bad weather, Southwest is hardly affected. They also make flying fun (at least for some people) and are able to rely on a very loyal customer base. Southwest is swimming in the Blue Ocean, or rather flying beyond the blue sky. Southwest and Cirque du Soleil exhibit the What, How, Why Balance. Consider again the Balanced Innovation Venn diagram.

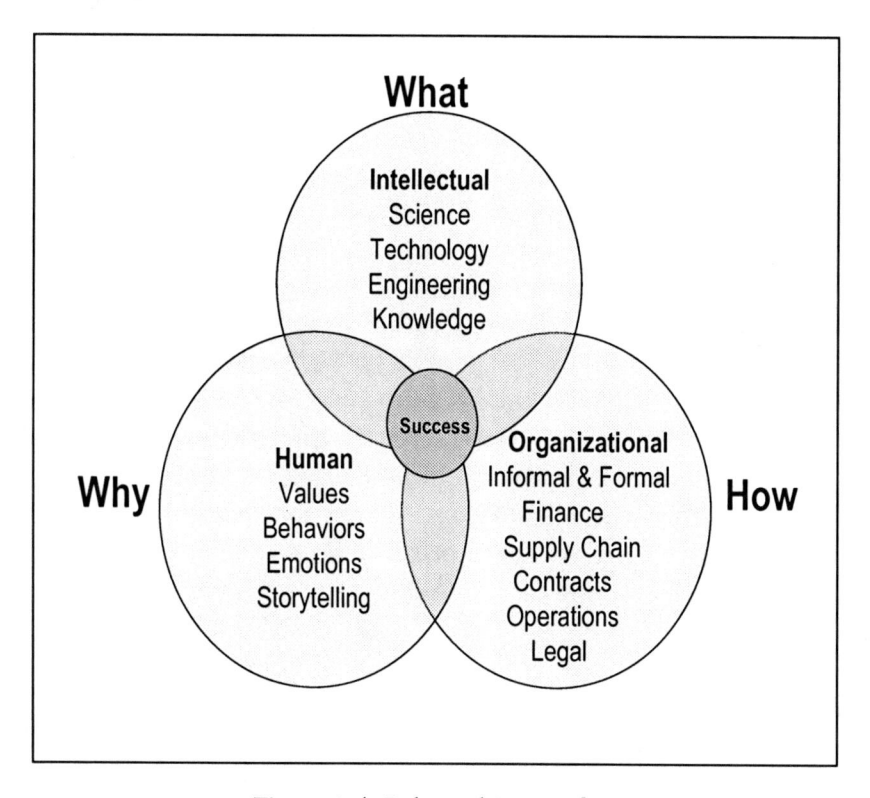

Figure 8.4. Balanced Innovation

The intellectual factors are What you do and What you know—your core competencies and strengths. The organizational factors are How you do it and How you learn. The human factors are Why you do it. What Southwest has become is a fun, reliable airline. How they do it is by providing point-to-point transportation with speed. Why they do it is to make airline travel available to everybody at a fraction of the cost and hassle of their contemporaries. The Southwest model is Balanced Innovation in every sense; they turn dreams into reality—

for themselves, their customers, and their shareholders. Southwest knows the What, the How, and the Why, and they never forget Who they are in business for.

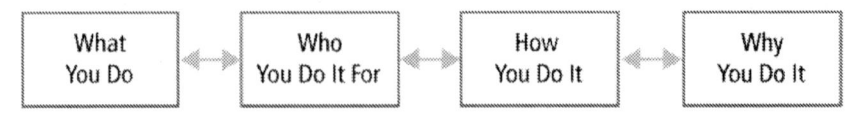

```
[What You Do] <-> [Who You Do It For] <-> [How You Do It] <-> [Why You Do It]
```

Figure 8.5. What, Who, How, and Why

Blended Growth

The old saying about not putting all your eggs in one basket is appropriate when considering whether to jump into the effective zone of all four sections of the growth quadrants. You need a blended approach to growth to ensure that you achieve your short-term targets while not ignoring mid- and long-term growth. You must continue to provide top-quality products and service to your existing customers. This ensures that as long as they have a need and there are no replacements for your offerings, customers will keep coming back to you. To maximize your capacity, you should also be looking for new customers for your existing products and services. You must continually keep your eyes and ears on the external environment as well, so that when there is a gap or customer need, you will recognize it. You must be creative in looking for ways to satisfy these needs, either with new offerings or revised versions of existing ones—whichever is appropriate for your customer.

If your current offerings are to become obsolete, isn't it better if it is your new offerings that make them obsolete? Now why didn't the Carters think of that?

In later chapters, we will look at how to listen to the "Chorus of the Customer" to help us identify and understand opportunities that will help move us into all four growth quadrants. Remember in chapter 3 we introduced the concept that the voice of the customer is really a chorus. Some customers sing the melody and others the harmony; in other words, there are decision makers and there are people who influence the decision makers. We also need to understand that the Chorus of the Customer is everywhere and always, and that business development is an activity and not just the name of a department. In other words, everybody is responsible for growth. We shall be discussing these ideas in more detail in the next few chapters.

In the meantime, here are a few (not so) random questions and thoughts about growth, for which I mean organic growth rather than growth through mergers and acquisitions. The relevance of Six Sigma is not coincidental!

» What is your major constraint to growth? Is it internal or external?
» How flexible is your organization? How receptive is it to change?
» What are the cultural impacts of a change toward a growth organization?
» Does your current sales force have the skills to work in the other three quadrants? Do these skills exist elsewhere in the organization?
» Developing a growth structure will require some or all of your commitment, passion, training, budget, process and infrastructure. Is your organization ready and willing to do this to grow?
» Is your organization willing and able to recruit top talent from outside?

In developing strategies to enable growth, it is important for you to address each of these questions in detail. For smaller organizations, commitment, passion, and a good process may suffice. Larger organizations may require all of the above. Do you have the appropriate ambition and energy? You could form a small team of peers (right- and left-brainers) to develop your strategies. The double-loop learning Six Sigma and 5-D models have been created to help in these efforts.

After assessing your thoughts and answers to these questions, look at your current offerings and the market you are working in and place each of your offerings in each of the four quadrants. Be as honest as you can about your evaluations. Most of your offerings will more than likely be firmly entrenched in the bottom left quadrant. Are you going to stay there, stuck in the mud of day-to-day competitive battle, or are you going to look at moving into the other three quadrants? Are you striving to achieve the What, How, Why Balance?

Developing New Business

An organization that is focused on growth recognizes that there are three stages when developing new business. Stage one is hunting for opportunities, where the customer may not yet have a need and the company may not have a product. Hunting involves understanding the environment; it is the art of ethnography—understanding where trends are going, finding what is missing that could become an opportunity for your company, and finding the white space (that flying green elephant again). Good hunting will help you find opportunities in all growth areas, including moving into the top right quadrant. Hunting for opportunities is about building relationships and developing trust.

Stage two is capture planning and win strategy-development, where a need has surfaced and you figure out how to develop a solution to satisfy that need. This is where Sony saw people exercising alongside mammoth music boxes in the 1980s, found a white space for portable music devices, and bridged the gap with the Walkman. The outcome from stage two will be a developed strategy and plan of action. The action plan will concentrate on key results that are required to move forward. It should ensure that constraints and barriers are overcome, and it should have a contact plan of people and organizations to approach. These could be customers, suppliers, and partners, or financial backers. Maybe the action plan includes a patent application, in which case a lawyer will be included in the contact plan. The win strategy needs to address the key elements required to turn the opportunity into new business.

Stage three is the proposal stage. You found the opportunity and designed a solution; now you have to make it so attractive that customers will buy it. This is where you tell your story. The outcome could be a proposal you have produced in answer to a request from a customer, or it could be a business plan where an entrepreneur approaches a bank or other venture capitalists for financial backing.

In a nutshell, the three stages are understand the need, develop the solution, and tell the story (see figure 8.6).

The choices of Six Sigma focus areas that I've shown in the three stages in figure 8.6 are based on my personal experience. You can use different focus areas as appropriate.

Hunting for Opportunities	Understand the need. **Focus Areas:** Identifying Customer Needs; With the Customer, for the Customer; Customer Engagement	Recognize gaps and find white-space opportunities.
Capture Planning/ Win Strategy-Development	Develop the solution. **Focus Areas:** Partnering, Defining Solutions, Increasing Customer Success	Assess the opportunity to establish solutions.
Proposal Development	Tell the story. **Focus Areas:** Increasing P Capture, Increasing Customer Success	Make the offering compelling. Make an emotional connection with your customers.

Figure 8.6. Winning Business

Success in moving from one stage to the next is dependent on the What, How, Why Balance. For reference, figure 8.7 shows again some examples of tools we can use in the focus areas.

Focus Area	Tools
Identifying Customer Needs	Listening, VOC, QFD, Brainstorming, Affinitization, Decision Tree, 5-Whys
With the Customer, for the customer	Tools dictated by the situation
Increasing Customer Success	Tools dictated by the situation
Partnering through the Value Chain	Tools dictated by the situation
Customer Engagement	Tools dictated by the situation
Growth Diagnosis	Process Maps, Critical Chain, Brainstorming, Root-Cause Analysis, 5-Whys, Affinitization
Defining Solutions	QFD, FMEA, Visioning, Brainstorming, TRIZ
Increasing P Capture	Critical Chain, Workshops, QFD, FMEA, Brainstorming, TRIZ

Figure 8.7. Six Sigma Growth Tools

Program X

I'd like to share a story about a program for which I have a great deal of personal attachment. It is a story that proves that the What, How, Why Balance between the intellectual, organizational, and human factors is vital to success. For the protection of the parties involved, we shall call this Program X. A few years ago I was a new business program manager for a UK company leading a team on a product that was basically on its last legs. We had tried and failed to penetrate the market for an upgraded faster, better, shinier version and were losing out to a new product from the United States. The British government, our main customer, was looking to replace our product with this new sexy version from across the Atlantic. We had to act fast.

We started by working with the customer to try to understand what their real needs were. We were looking for areas where even the new U.S. product might have a weakness; in effect, we were looking for gaps. Fortunately, even though the new offering from overseas outperformed our ancient product, we discovered a few gaps in capability (both real and imaginary) and looked for opportunities to exploit them. Next we conducted a series of "operational scenario" tests to see how important these gaps in capability might be. In the operational scenario tests, we attempted to reconstruct lifelike conditions to see how different conditions would affect the outcomes. Of course, we designed the tests specifically to ensure that our goal was achieved and we highlighted several gaps in capability. Armed with these results, we sought out supporters in the government. These early advocates were the key messengers in spreading the word about the potential problems of buying from overseas. Some of the problems were technical; some were related to political considerations; most were real, and some were imaginary. All the issues were designed to solidify our emotional advantage. Eventually the government conceded that neither our ancient product, nor the shiny new one from America, was going to fully meet their operational requirements. We were developing our emotional connections to validate the What, How, Why Balance.

The customer created a new requirement for Program X, and they invited both companies to compete for this lucrative opportunity.

This true story is a terrific example of hunting for opportunities in action. It was as much about creating an opportunity as it was hunting for one. We had expanded the playing field and were now in the game. Obviously, being in the game doesn't guarantee you are going to be successful; our competitor was still the strong favorite to win the contract. After all, their original offering was close to what the customer needed. Unlike us, they didn't need to start from a blank sheet of paper.

During the win strategy-development phase, we had to find ways to make our offering compelling to further build the emotional connections with our customer. We also had to eliminate the major cost advantage our competitors had over us. What did we do? We turned our solution into a European one. We teamed with the leading European companies in our field to provide the best solution that Europe could offer. Our new teammates heavily lobbied their governments to support a joint European solution. We had funding promises from each government that blew away the price advantage of the U.S. competitor.

The proposal phase had some interesting challenges, as we sought to satisfy the needs of the French, German, Italian, Spanish, and Swedish partners. Thankfully, the final reward was worth it: our team was awarded a $1.5 billion contract.

We worked with the Chorus of the Customer (see chapter 9), made everybody on the team responsible for developing the business, and then made our competitor irrelevant. We bridged the Innovation Gap intellectually, organizationally, and emotionally. Nobody accused us of making it easy for ourselves, but the final reward spoke for itself.

I have been asked several times how we managed to win Program X. I believe it is because we had a balanced approach. At all stages of the competition, the What, How, and Why validated one another. We could never claim that our technology was better, and our solution was probably more of a technical risk than that of our U.S. competitor. So we made sure that our story addressed this in a positive way. Furthermore, we had an organizational approach that made it easy for the customer to do business with us. We also had a human approach that made strong, positive emotional connections with the people in the customer community who made the decisions. Our competitor, by contrast, relied on a low-risk technical solution and focused on the members of the customer community who gave them the answers they wanted to hear. Fortunately for us, the U.S. competitor was anything but balanced.

In striving to find balance in proposals, it is essential to eradicate the vital lies and limiting assumptions. Try using a stakeholder grid where you assess who in the customer community is your advocate or adversary, who is an opponent or a fair-weather friend, and who may still be sitting on the fence. A stakeholder grid is a simple two-by-two matrix that provides a quick idea of the position of the key stakeholders as supporters, opponents, fair-weather friends, or adversaries. If the decision makers are adversaries and their key influencers aren't too supportive either, you can try to change their opinions through your behavior, which is often very difficult, or you can invest in a different pursuit.

Why We Win and Why We Lose

I have studied over thirty major proposals in various industries and found that the root cause behind success and failure is very revealing. In all successful proposals, a strong What, How, Why Balance existed between the intellectual, organizational, and human factors. In all cases, the winning team engaged early with the customer and forged strong, positive emotional connections. The winning team developed solutions to reflect the real human needs of the customer and created a compelling, easy-to-understand proposal story. Customer relationships are strong and based on mutual trust. The winning team is always organized to make it easy for the customer to place the contract, knowing with confidence that the team has the ability and desire to deliver the desired outcome.

By contrast, unsuccessful proposals are weak in one or more of these areas, causing an imbalance between the What, How and Why of the intellectual, organizational and human factors. Here are some examples.

Intellectually Weak proposals usually reveal a higher price than the competition, a higher risk, or a combination of both. There may be elements of noncompliance as well, where the solution offered didn't fully meet the needs of the customer. In all cases, a flawed strategy also reflects a weak emotional connection with the key decision makers in the customer community, often through late engagement, lack of empathy, or both. In most cases, it is not the technical capability of the solution per se that has lost the proposal.

Organizationally Weak proposals often involve a suboptimal capture team with team members who are lacking some of the necessary skills and experience. There is often too much churning of proposal staff, including the key members of the team. The informal network is usually stifled in some way with failing cross-functional communication. Teaming is often late and not strategic, and it doesn't fill the perceived gaps in a way that builds customer confidence.

Proposals that are weak on the **Human** side often reflect a late engagement with the customer as well. There are weak relationships with key decision makers and other influencers. There may be a perception of poor past performance that hasn't been corrected. The customer believes that the organization didn't understand their needs, didn't listen, and didn't speak their language.

All of these weaknesses reflect a lack of positive emotional connections with key members of the customer community, resulting in a lack of trust, a lack of understanding, and an inability or lack of desire to address the real needs and desires. Customers often buy emotionally and then justify the decision with logic. Winning proposals reflect this, but unsuccessful proposals do not.

Successful proposals almost exclusively exhibit the What, How, Why Balance, and unsuccessful proposals almost exclusively do not.

Good Growth

A final thought on growth is that there may be bad growth as well as good growth. Growth that adversely affects the return on invested capital (ROIC) of a company is bad growth. ROIC is the net operating profit of an organization, divided by the investment made by shareholders plus equity and assets. The higher the ROIC, the better the shareholders will feel. Certain mergers and acquisitions have led to bad growth as huge debts are created and the investors subsequently lose confidence. A Six Sigma analysis of alternatives using risk mitigation tools like a FMEA (Failure Mode Effects Analysis) can be very useful. A FMEA is a systematic technique used to identify potential failures and then prioritize those failures in terms of severity, occurrence probability, and probability of detection. In general, Six Sigma projects have focused on the bottom line. This helps increase net operating profits through efficiencies and the reduction of variation and waste. Six Sigma for Innovations and Growth is focused on top-line growth, as well by increasing profits through the winning of new business. Make sure you focus on good growth; it has the right What, How, Why Balance.

Do you feel passionate about the needs of your customers and the opportunities these needs present? Are you changing the playing field? Do you have a balanced approach to Innovation to enable you to grow into adjacent markets? Do you recognize where there may be opportunities to move into all the quadrants?

Key Points in Chapter 8

- » The growth matrix has four quadrants where growth can occur.
- » Working with and listening to the customer is key to organic growth.
- » Learn how to cure your customers' insomnia.
- » Balanced Innovation provides new opportunities for growth.
- » Balanced Innovation is key to success in a competitive world.
- » Developing a growth structure requires commitment and passion.
- » Organizations grow business opportunities in three stages: hunting for opportunities, capture planning/win strategy-development, and proposals.
- » Use your discretionary budgets wisely. Regularly assess the What, How, Why Balance, and make knowledge-based decisions on which pursuits to invest in.
- » Successful proposals exhibit the What, How, Why Balance; unsuccessful proposals do not.
- » There is bad growth as well as good growth. Focus on good growth.
- » Good growth has the right What, How, Why Balance.

Key Questions to Ask Yourself

- » What do you plan to do to ignite your personal growth?
- » How can you change the game to make the emotional connections your customers expect? Are you listening?
- » What is the major constraint or barrier to growth? Is it internal or external? How are you planning to overcome this constraint or barrier?
- » How flexible is the organization? How receptive is it to change? Can you articulate how change is good for growth?
- » How will you ensure your next proposals have the right What, How, Why Balance?

- » What are the cultural impacts of a change toward a growth organization?
- » Does the current sales force have the skills to move out of their comfort zone and work in the other three quadrants? If not, why not? What can you do about it?

chapter 9

the chorus of the customer

The human factors of the What, How, Why Balance will make or break a new product launch or proposal. A major aspect of this is your relationships with key customers. However, the customer base is often diverse and even disparate. So how do we get the real voice of the customer (VOC)? VOC has become very vogue in recent times, but in most cases the customer has more than one voice; there, is in fact, a Chorus of the Customer. Robin Lawton suggests in his book *Creating a Customer-Centered Culture* that we categorize customers into users, fixers, and brokers. In my experience, there are other influencers as well, such as Congress and lawmakers, banks, and other sources of funding. It is useful to know which of these customers has the power—in other words, who is singing the melody and who is singing the harmony? Another way to categorize is the people who make the decisions and the people who influence the people making the decisions. Once you understand who has the power, you can create and develop strategies to build the right kind of relationships. Relationships with our customers are not only key; they are vital. Here are a few questions you could ponder to establish a baseline:

» Customer Profile Overview
» Who is the customer? What are his or her needs and wants?
» Customer Assessment
» What do you know about your customer, from a business and personal viewpoint? What is the name of the customer's spouse or partner?
» Competitor Assessment
    What relationship does your customer have with your competition?

- » Company Assessment
  What is your position and image with the customer? Do you have an emotional connection with your customer? What image does your competition have?
- » Customer Relationship
  Do you/are you listening to your customers? What are they telling you?
- » Customer Cares
  What are the customer's concerns, worries, and hot buttons?
- » Partnering Plan
  How do you work with the customer to resolve his or her concerns and worries?

It is so important to listen to our customers. Treat them as you would any other conversational partner, and really try to understand their hot buttons before presenting your offerings. The two may not match, and the customer will know whether or not you have his or her interests at heart. When conversing, try to see the customer's point of view from his or her biography, not your own autobiography. Learn empathic listening, where you see the world the way your conversational partner sees it. This way you can build a trusted relationship and be seen as a solution provider and problem solver. It's amazing how this will lead to new opportunities.

Several of the Six Sigma focus areas are applicable here: Identifying Customer Needs; With the Customer, for the Customer; Customer Engagement; and Increasing Customer Success. These focus areas are designed to provide high-quality, early VOC.

In order to become a solutions provider, we need to understand the outputs and outcomes the customer is seeking. Consider a racing car. If we were product oriented, as most of us are, we would provide a car with the most horsepower and best technical specification. But that may not suit the customers' needs. They want the car to go as fast as possible under all conditions—in other words, they want the car to generate excitement. But that, too, is useless if they never win a race because the car is unreliable or requires too many pit stops for fuel and tire changes. The outcome required is to win the race and win the championship. So in developing the car, we need to understand all the tangibles and intangibles, from the gleam in a customer's eye to the final success as the championship garland is placed over the driver's head. To achieve this requires the right What, How, Why Balance. Figure 9.1 reminds us how using the focus areas might flow over time.

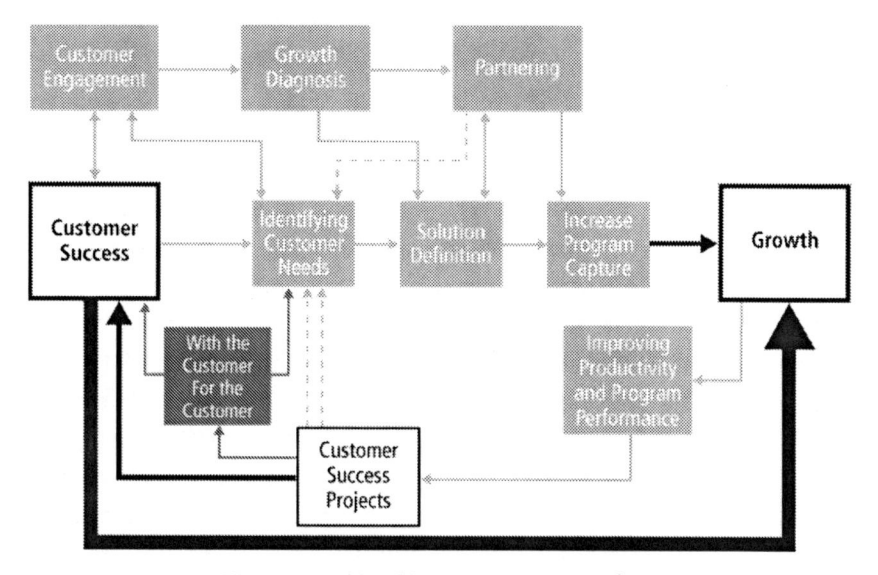

Figure 9.1. Six Sigma Focus Area Flow

The House of Quality tool, the quality function deployment (QFD),[1] is very useful here. As a reminder, the QFD provides a systematic approach to understanding and prioritizing customer needs and desires into the key discriminators. It forces conversations about needs, wants, and wows. The best use of a QFD always takes place when the customer is present and helping to input the data. A QFD can help validate the What, How, Why Balance.

The Chorus of the Customer often involves conflict. For example, the current needs of the broker may not be aligned to the current needs of the fixer or user. You will need to be able to recognize that

---

1   A flexible and comprehensive group decision-making technique used in product or service development, brand marketing, and product management.

there is a conflict (no vital lies, please), understand it, and find ways to manage it. With Program X, we discovered incredible conflict among the various departments in the British government. Many of the brokers didn't want the hassle of having to create a new requirement and the inevitable delays that would follow. So we took baby steps: first we found advocates in the user community, made an emotional connection with them, and then we supported their passion as they spread the advocacy. In my experience, passion outweighs indifference by a factor of at least 10:1.

Another useful tool to use in assessing how focused you are on your customers is the value chain.[2] You can use a value chain as an external look at your competitive position. Do your assets and core competencies match your customers' priorities? Your core competencies and strengths are things you do well—what your customer expects from your organization. Core competencies and strengths are the things that give your organization a competitive edge. What are your company's strengths? Do you deliver your strengths throughout your experience with your customer? Can you tailor your core strengths and competencies to match your customers' priorities? A traditional tool like a value chain can be useful in understanding how balanced your Innovation might be and how well it matches your customers' expectations.

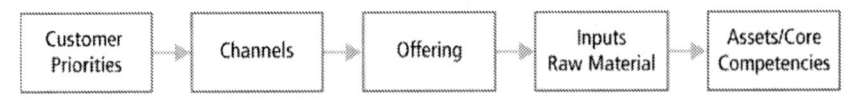

| Customer Priorities | → | Channels | → | Offering | → | Inputs Raw Material | → | Assets/Core Competencies |

Figure 9.2 Value Chain

Try to ensure you understand the Chorus of the Customer, especially what their needs and desires are, before offering solutions. Who has the power, both now and in the future, and how are you going to capture what is important to them? Where are your passionate advo-

---

2   Strategic look at the key links in the chain between customer needs and an organization's core competencies. First made popular by Michael Porter in *Competitive Advantage: Creating and Sustaining Superior Performance.*

cates, and how do you fuel their fire with a strong, positive emotional connection? It is also very important to know how their decisions are made, who makes them, and who influences the decision makers. Prove you understand their needs through your behavior, and tell your joint story in the customers' words. Take time to understand these key factors, and you will reap the rewards.

Key Points in Chapter 9

- » The voice of the customer is in fact a chorus.
- » The customer base is wide and diverse.
- » Understanding who has the power is key to achieving the What, How, Why Balance.
- » Relationships are vital.
- » Understand what outcomes your customers are looking for.
- » The QFD tool is a good way to prioritize customer needs and desires.
- » QFD can help validate the What, How, Why Balance.
- » Six Sigma increases the potential for success.
- » A Value Chain can help confirm the balance of your Innovation.
- » Prove that you understand the needs of the customer through your behaviors, and tell your joint story in their words.

Key Questions to Ask Yourself

- » Who is the customer, and what are his/her needs and wants? How are you currently satisfying them? How can you really delight this customer?
- » What do you know about your customer, from a business and personal viewpoint? What is the name of the customer's spouse or partner?
- » What relationship does your customer have with the competition? Is it better than your relationship? If yes, why? How can you make this customer become totally devoted to you?
- » What is your position and image with the customer? What image does your competition have? How can you improve your image?
- » Do you/are you listening to your customers? What are they telling you? What do you do with the information they share with you?
- » What are the customer's concerns, worries, and hot buttons? How can you solve these issues and problems?
- » How do you work with the customer to resolve his or her

concerns and worries? Is there a better way of working together? What are you going to do about it?
» What can you do to better your relationship with your customer?
» How can you get a positive emotional connection with your customer?

chapter 10

the chorus is everywhere and always

Another important aspect of the Chorus of the Customer is that it is everywhere and always. This is irrespective of the nature of your business. You are always on duty, and your personal, professional, and business brand can be positively or negatively affected at any time. Even the most menial of questions from a customer during a phone call can make a huge difference if answered positively and quickly. Be careful how you behave at all times; remember that you are being judged by your behavior and not your values. One useful rule is to remember that whenever you meet, speak to, think about, talk about, or otherwise engage with a customer or other important person in your life, it presents an opportunity. You can either seize it, let it go, or kill it. The world is shrinking, and you never know who you are sitting next to in a restaurant or on an airplane. I have lost count of the times I have been speaking with somebody for the first time to find out we have a mutual friend or acquaintance. And that acquaintance is often your customer.

Channels Strategy

Once you accept that the chorus is everywhere and always, you need to establish a strategy for channeling the information you receive to the appropriate department or person. Capturing the customer viewpoint is irrelevant if you do nothing with it. A well thought-out and executed Channels Strategy can make a huge difference to you and your customers.

A Channels Strategy is simply a means of turning early VOC information into new business opportunities by channeling it to the department or area that can take appropriate action. This can lead to ideas that transform customer satisfaction into growth opportunities. A good example of Channels Strategy is at Disney, where every one of their thousands of custodial staff members are sensors for customer feedback.

What would a well thought-out Channels Strategy look like? Firstly, it needs to have a simple capture method. Find a way where the information can easily be passed on. Have a process and methodology that is easy and not bureaucratic. Find a way of getting feedback to the person who sends in the message or idea, even if it is to say no. If you can't act, make sure the originator understands why. The last thing you need is to kill the information supply because you didn't have time to explain your reason. However, on those marvelous occasions when the idea creates an opportunity, execute! Don't continue to make those buggy whips. Figure 10.1 shows how a Channels Strategy process might look.

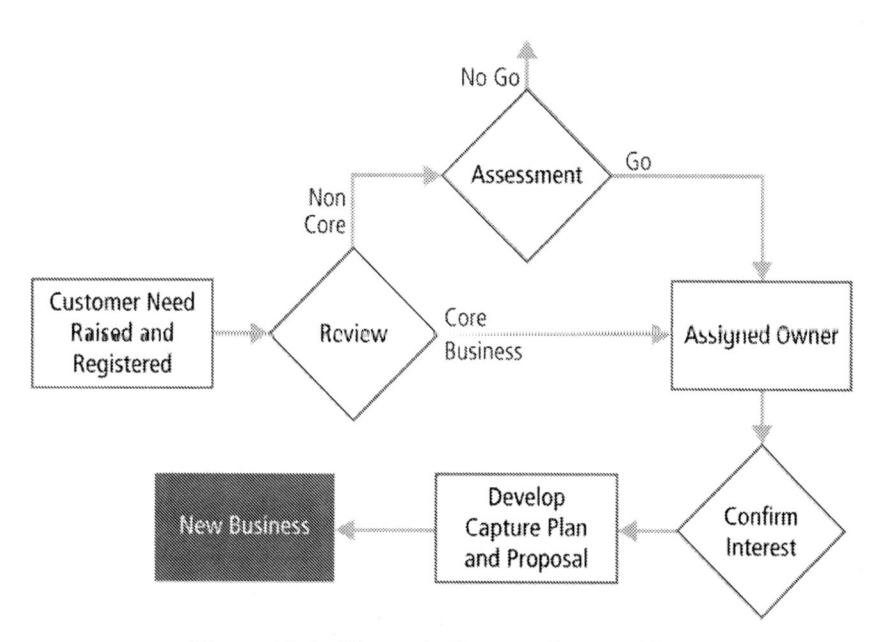

Figure 10.1. Channels Strategy Process Flow

Once a customer need has been identified, it is assessed as either core business or non core business. If it is non core, your organization will need to decide if it is a business area you want to move into. If the customer need is considered worth pursuing further, an owner needs to be assigned. The owner then has the responsibility for forming a team of subject matter experts who can help develop the opportunity. After further investigation and additional discussions with the customer, you will either confirm interest or, if the opportunity doesn't look attractive enough to pursue, decide that no further action is required. Assuming a positive review, the organization is committed and will move into the Capture phase in preparation for the Proposal phase . This works whether you are in the restaurant business and looking to add a new location or a high-technology firm looking to grow with new product offerings. A Channels Strategy is also a useful method to establish better ways to serve your customers. Good customer and competitive intelligence is essential for any business that needs or wants to grow. A Channels Strategy process enables businesses to better understand their markets and environment, and it is a useful tool in all areas of the growth matrix shown again in figure 10.2.

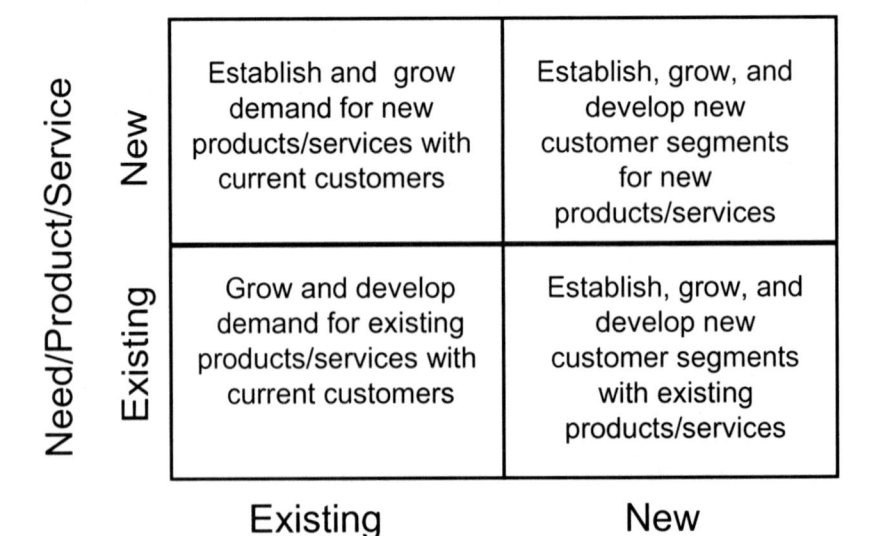

	Existing Customer	New Customer
Need/Product/Service New	Establish and grow demand for new products/services with current customers	Establish, grow, and develop new customer segments for new products/services
Need/Product/Service Existing	Grow and develop demand for existing products/services with current customers	Establish, grow, and develop new customer segments with existing products/services

Figure 10.2. Where Growth Occurs

Channels Strategy is another great way to validate the What, How, Why Balance. Successful execution will enable you to understand the current state of the customer's thinking and needs. But more importantly, it helps drive the organization toward the desired future state of delighted customers and business growth.

CEOs and other business leaders are telling us to improve our performance in the eyes of our customer and to develop stronger relationships. Success in these areas will help develop trust, and when they trust you, you become the go-to guy to help solve their problems. Ken Blanchard has written many books on this subject, including *Raving Fans* which he co-authored with Sheldon Bowles. Harry Beckwith's best-selling book *Selling the Invisible* also provides many great thoughts on the subject. Both these books discuss the little details that help keep customers loyal.

A well-executed Channels Strategy helps create those "raving fans." It also provides a terrific insertion point for Innovation. The front end of Innovation is the creative ideation phase. If this creativity is focused on customer needs, you are already on the way to achieving the What, How, Why Balance required for success.

Let's take an example where a high-tech company has a number of field service representatives working full-time at the customers' premises. The primary purpose of the field service representatives is to keep a sophisticated product in service and available for customers' use. One day a customer suggests that although the product is high tech and provides value, it is difficult to use and half the features are never operated. The report goes in from the field representative to the program manager who has overall responsibility for the product. The program manager then consults the broker who manages the equipment for the customer, and a meeting is set up between the interested parties. The outcome is simple: the company provides a low-cost modification to change the operation. This generates immediate revenue and customer delight. The new modifications are then incorporated into the design, and as a result, the price comes down. This generates additional customers who benefit from the new easy-to-use device. Word starts to spread and our customer base becomes our biggest and best group of marketers.

In the meantime, the Channels Strategy process includes the

ability to monitor all the ideas that are generated. They are displayed on a dashboard like the one shown in figure 10.3.

Number Of Ideas In 06	Number Implemented	Contracts Generated	Revenue To Date	Potential Future Revenue
64	21	15	$28M	$130M

Figure 10.3. Channel Strategy Dashboard

The CEO is happy because she can see how well the Channels Strategy is working and how much the company is growing as a direct result.

More detailed dashboards can be made available to suit the needs of vice presidents and product line managers.

Reward is important, and this can take many forms. Not all rewards have to be monetary, but obviously a cash incentive is always nice. Something as simple as a personal thank-you can be very effective. My advice is to make sure you celebrate your successes.

My first introduction to a Channels Strategy was when I led a Six Sigma project to address a huge burning platform. Why was one of our major competitors announcing new contracts before we even knew there was a need? We were often getting first indications from our frontline field engineers but did nothing with the information. Thus, we asked, "How can we better use our frontline resources like field engineers to provide better quality, early customer and competitor intelligence?"

This was a major project, and we started with a growth diagnosis to identify root causes. The main problem was that our field engineers didn't know who to send reports to. Even when they did send in a report, it was often ignored or didn't get channeled to the appropriate resource for action. We developed solutions, created a simple-to-use process, and reversed the situation to such an extent that our competitor didn't know what hit them. Customer delight increased, and we were offering solutions that were balanced. Channels Strategy works!

Having a Channels Strategy is ethnography in action. It is totally customer focused. The frontline representatives are equally as important to the customer as they are to the company. It is these frontline representatives who make the emotional connection with your customers, each and every day. Disney and the Ritz-Carlton get most of their customer feedback through their custodial cast members and staff. It can work for anybody, from mom-and-pop pizza delivery franchises to an organization as big and complex as Disney.

Positive behavior that reflects the needs and desires of the customer is a key strength, and Channels Strategy is all about positive behavior. A well-executed Channels Strategy will enable you to make strong emotional connections with your customers. The reward will be an elevation of your brand and many new opportunities for business. It can kick-start Innovation. A good Channels Strategy will be simple. It has to allow your frontline personnel to easily communicate, even from the most remote of places. A Channels Strategy should not be bureaucratic. Are you taking the hassle out of your customers' lives? By making their lives uncomplicated, they can focus on their priorities. This is customer focus in action. If you do it right, you make those positive emotional connections, they will be successful, and your company will grow.

A final thought on the chorus being everywhere and always. We have six senses, including the not-very-common common sense. Unfortunately, we tend to use only our sense of hearing. Use the other senses as appropriate when dealing with any other human you come into contact with. Body language and the strength of a handshake can often tell you much more than verbal communication.

You can turn your current dissatisfied customers into satisfied ones and satisfied customers into delighted ones. When you delight customers often enough, they will become raving fans and the greatest advocates you can have. Advocacy among customers will spread and help generate new opportunities. They will become more willing to share their issues and thoughts with you because trust has increased. This will generate more opportunities. Just like success, customer advocacy is contagious.

Key Points in Chapter 10

- » The customer is everywhere and always.
- » Make sure you seize the opportunities you are presented with.
- » The front end of Innovation is the ideation phase. By focusing this on customer needs, success should follow.
- » Fuel your Innovations by implementing a Channels Strategy.
- » An easy-to-use Channels Strategy process will make a very positive difference.
- » A well-executed Channels Strategy validates the What, How, Why Balance.
- » A Six Sigma project can help develop a successful Channels Strategy.
- » Use all your senses when conversing.
- » Make common sense more common.

Key Questions to Ask Yourself

- » What do you do with the information you receive from your frontline representatives?
- » How do you seize the opportunities presented to you? If you don't, why not?
- » Do you have a simple and easy-to-use Channels Strategy? What action can you take to develop one?
- » Are you the go-to guy for your customers? Is there an emotional connection?
- » What can you do to become the trusted partner for your customers?
- » How passionate are you about becoming their trusted partner?
- » How can you help your frontline representatives provide early, high-quality information that will fuel the Channels Strategy on a regular basis?

chapter 11

business development is an activity, not just a department's name

Just as the customer is everywhere and always, business development is the responsibility of everybody in an organization. Everybody should be customer focused. If you are not doing something directly for the customer, you should be supporting somebody who is. Human resources should have growth strategies that include recruiting and keeping the best appropriate talent. Finance should be finding creative legal ways to fund projects, engineering should be designing for the customer and not just because the project is an interesting challenge, program managers should be relentlessly focused on helping their customers be successful, IT should be focused on simple, easy-to-use systems to help management and enable customer success … you get the picture! Of course, this includes using Six Sigma and Lean techniques to ensure processes are effective, fast, and efficient. This will reduce and avoid costs, and allow the savings to be reinvested.

If everybody understands the What, How, Why Balance and works toward customer success, you will have an amazing business-development multiplier. Useful ideas will promulgate, fueling the front end of Innovation.

Let's refer again to the eight Six Sigma focus areas (shown again in figure 11.1). Each of these focus areas uses methods such as workshops, blitzes, visioning, and brainstorming. These sessions are more successful when a diverse team of subject matter experts (SMEs) participates—especially a team that includes a good mix of both right-brain and left-brain thinkers.

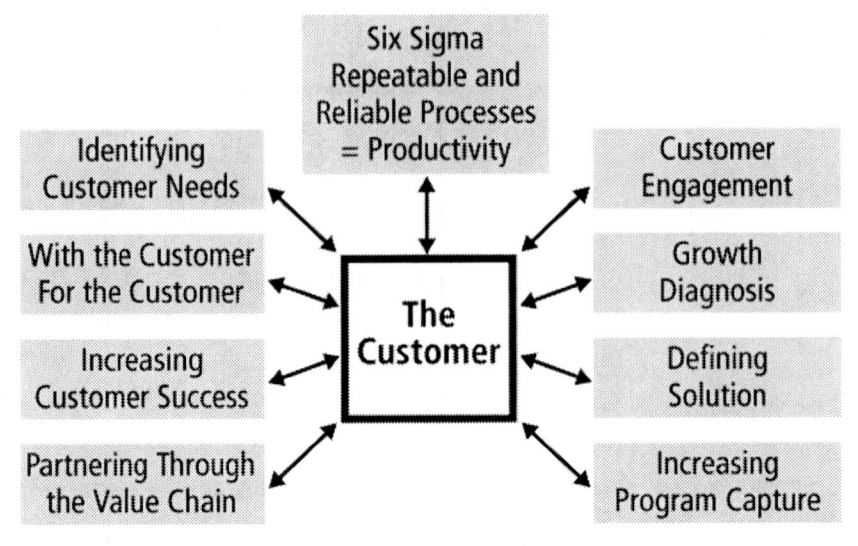

```
                Six Sigma
              Repeatable and
              Reliable Processes
  Identifying   = Productivity      Customer
Customer Needs    ↑                 Engagement
         ↘        │        ↗
With the Customer                   Growth
For the Customer       ┌─────────┐  Diagnosis
         ↘    ↔        │  The    │ ↔
                       │Customer │
  Increasing           │         │  Defining
Customer Success       └─────────┘  Solution
         ↗        │        ↘
Partnering Through                  Increasing
the Value Chain                     Program Capture
```

Figure 11.1. Six Sigma Growth Focus Areas

If business development is treated as an activity and not just a department, work becomes more fun and growth follows. Here are a few business development competencies that should flow throughout an organization that is intent on Innovation and revenue.

» **Strategic Marketing.** Develop and execute successful business growth strategies. This includes understanding the outcomes that will show success and understanding which markets are desirable. Does the strategy have enough emotional resonance to generate the required passion for success? Does the strategy involve an executable communications plan? Can the strategy be easily described? A strategy without implementation is merely a dream. Make sure the strategy is communicated and understood. The growth diagnosis focus area is very useful here. Six Sigma tools and methods can be used to help in the new business investment decision-making process. Do your organization's strategies and business models reflect the needs of the external environment? Do you really understand the current state of the external environment on both a macro and micro level? Has the marketplace changed, creating a change in your circumstances that affects the What, How, Why Balance? To understand the current state, look again at the outer loop of the double-loop learning model shown in figure 11.2 (next page).

» **Company Knowledge.** A good understanding of the company is important, especially in larger companies, to be able to leverage enterprise-wide solutions that will create raving fans. Can you find intersections between different areas of the company? Can you bring together these differences to develop customer-based solutions? Also, when you meet with a customer, they look to you as a representative of that company, not just of a particularly product. Wear the company's name as proudly as you wear your own name. Are you using your frontline personnel to bring early customer intelligence?

» **Solutions Oriented.** Use the 5-D process to ensure solutions that meet or exceed the customer's needs and desires.

» **Relationship Focused.** Everybody, everywhere, should use personal influence to nurture and maintain positive internal and external relationships to benefit the business. This is one of the most important competencies for any successful person—and not just in developing business. Use your social capital. If you don't have any in a certain area or circumstance, borrow somebody else's who does.

» **Positive Energy.** Do you and your fellow leaders demonstrate passion (there's the P word again), savviness, and sensitivity to leverage relationships and achieve results?

Understanding these competencies will provide a major competitive advantage. It is equally important that you have the knowledge to be able to think strategically and act tactically to turn a dream into reality. Consider again the double-loop learning model shown in figure 11.2.

Any outside influence can affect a strategy, and early high-quality warnings of changes can mean the difference between success and failure—hence the benefits of a Channels Strategy to provide high-quality, early competitive intelligence! Using frontline staff for VOC

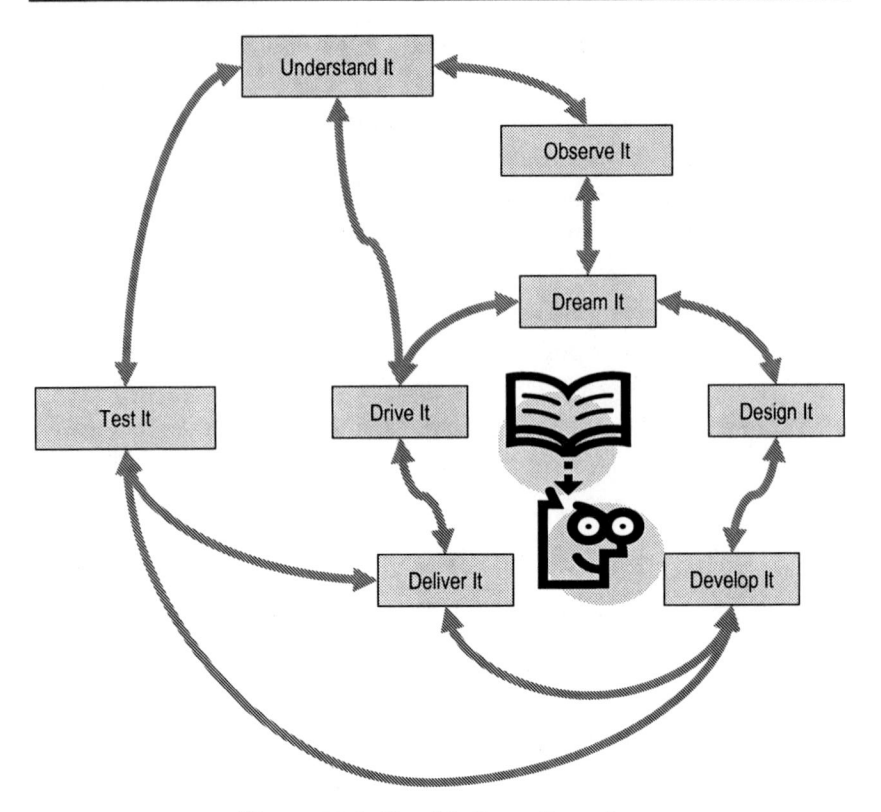

Figure 11.2. Double-Loop Learning

inputs is another business development multiplier. Let's pick on my ancestors again and their obsession with the buggy whip. When the Carters found out about the potential of the automobile, it was already too late and then its impact wasn't understood. Then the threat to the business was denied through a series of vital lies, until finally the buggy whip became an irrelevance because the buggy became an irrelevance.

Here are some attributes that an organization focused on growth should aspire to.

- » Understand what your customers are looking for from you.
- » Understand how procurement decisions are made by your customers.
- » Know which customers have the power.
- » Work at many levels in the customer's organization.
- » Work at many levels within your company.

- » Be perceptive enough to recognize customers' evolving needs.
- » Communicate evolving needs without distortion.
- » Get the organization to act quickly and appropriately.
- » Spot the gaps—the unwritten, unspoken, white space needs.

Simple attributes to understand! In a larger organization, the various SMEs can share the attributes. Small organizations will have a level of intimacy with the customer, and one or two key individuals probably share these attributes. It is useful here to imagine that the word *TEAM* is an acronym standing for Together Everyone Achieves More, as cited by many leaders and even displayed on a Successories poster.

Teamwork can help develop the What, How, Why Balance. If the buggy whip manufacturers had listened to the team members who understood the changes taking shape in the marketplace, they would have had more data and could have made different decisions. These different knowledge-based decisions may have led to new product offerings for the automobile. The Carter's buggy whips were the best in the world, and the Carters knew what to do and how to do it; they just forgot the reason why. When Mercedes and Ford produced better alternatives to the buggy, the Carter's buggy whip supremacy was over. The external environment had significantly changed the What, How, Why Balance.

Key Points in Chapter 11

- » Business development is the responsibility of everybody in an organization.
- » A culture focused on the What, How, Why Balance creates a business development multiplier.
- » Being able to think strategically and act tactically is a competitive advantage.
- » Marketing needs to be strategic, communicated, and understood.
- » Being relationship focused is key; use personal influence and social capital.
- » Develop an integrated social network.
- » Borrow social capital from others when appropriate.
- » Demonstrate passion and positive energy.

Key Questions to Ask Yourself

- » How does your company encourage you to create an environment for employees to think proactively about developing business? Or do you rely on your sales department?
- » How do you make sure that you understand what your customers are looking for from their suppliers?
- » How are procurement decisions made by your customer?
- » Which customers have the power, and who may be wasting your time?
- » Can you work comfortably at many levels in the customer's organization?
- » How do you work comfortably at many levels in your own company?
- » Are you perceptive enough to recognize customers' evolving needs? How do you find out what the customers' evolving needs are?
- » How do you communicate evolving needs without distortion (from your customer's perspective and not from within your own autobiography)?

- » Can you get the organization to act quickly and appropriately to ensure that you are ahead of the game?
- » Can you spot the gaps—the unwritten, unspoken, white space needs?
- » What can you do to improve your position in these areas?
- » Has the external environment changed your What, How, Why Balance?

chapter 12

love the customer

It is an obvious thing to say, but loving the customer is not as commonplace as you might imagine. Believe it or not, some people regard their customers as an inconvenience. How can these people ever understand that relentless customer focus leads to customer success and that customer success leads to growth and shareholder value? How can they validate the What, How, Why Balance of the intellectual, organizational, and human factors that are so vital for Innovation and revenue growth? If we make our customers and the customers of our customers successful, we will all benefit. But we need to do it with a firm grip on reality and constant attention to the relationship. If we are totally devoted to making our customers successful but are painful to deal with, they may go elsewhere next time. If we regularly say "no because," they will go elsewhere. But if we are focused on relationships and customer success, they will likely never consider changing suppliers. If we respond with a yes, they will keep coming back for more. Trust is huge. If they know they can trust you, it is unlikely they will risk an alternative.

Love has been recognized as a powerful emotion throughout history. It often surpasses the strength of all other emotions in terms of its impact and effect. There is a teaching engraved on the Sphinx that states "Love is the secret of life." In the caves of the Anchorites near Mount Sinai, it is written "Love and Wisdom, is the secret of life." On the doorway of the great rock near Deir, Petraea, it is engraved "The torch of life is fed by the oil of love." A famous Stoic sage once commanded "Love everything that happens to you."[1]

---

1 For these and other quotes on love, see *Wisdom of the Mystic Masters* by Joseph J. Weed.

Love your family. Love the things you are doing. Love each minute of every day. Love your job, love your coworkers, love your suppliers, and love your customers. If you don't, you may want to consider making some major life changes.

Here are a few sentences you could try completing.
» I love my customer because …
» I love what my customer does because …
» I love making my customer successful because …

Completing these sentences in an honest way will reveal why you do what you do. What makes you crave success? It will also show you where your passions are. Try answering the same questions about your boss, your partner, your current project, your job, your coworkers, and your suppliers. Love is a key enabler in the What, How, Why Balance because it validates the human factors with the intellectual and organizational aspects.

Retaining current customers is so much easier than cultivating new ones. Authors Ken Blanchard and Sheldon Bowles talk about making our customers "raving fans." Why don't you become "raving fans" of your customers as well?

Loyalty is something that cannot and must not ever be overrated. The customer is not an inconvenience, and neither are your coworkers. If you love your customers and your coworkers, you will have strong, positive emotional connections with them. Ask what you should be doing to help your customers stay loyal. Host a Six Sigma blitz around this issue. Focus the blitz on achieving the What, How, Why Balance.

By loving your customers, you will develop relationships where you become the go-to guy. Customers will ask you questions and share their concerns in a way that will open up more opportunities, simply because of the respect and trust they have for you. These opportunities can spark Innovation. Turning opportunity into reality is Innovation in action because you are introducing something new that adds value. Having a simple-to-use Channels Strategy, as discussed in chapter 10, will help you get the opportunity or idea to the person or function that can devote the right skills and energy to developing it. This is the What, How, Why Balance of Innovation.

Key Points in Chapter 12

- » Loving your customer is a competitive advantage.
- » Loving your customer validates the What, How, Why Balance that is so essential for Innovation and growth.
- » Love everything you do every day.
- » Relentless customer focus leads to customer success.
- » Customer success leads to growth.
- » Your customers are not an inconvenience.
- » Understand the reasons you love your customer to find your passions.
- » Loyalty to your customers and your coworkers should never be overrated.
- » Host a Six Sigma blitz addressing customer loyalty.

Key Questions to Ask Yourself

- » Do you love your customer? Are you his or her biggest fan? Why?
- » Do you have a strong, positive emotional connection with your customer? How?
- » Are you doing everything you can to make your customer successful?
- » What else should you be doing to keep your customers loyal?
- » How can you help your customers love you?

chapter 13

irrelevantize the competition

Okay let's admit it: the word *irrelevantize* has been made up, but it should be a real word (if Merriam is reading, please help). The fact is that too many businesses focus too heavily on their competition—what are they doing, who they are doing it with, let's undercut their price, or let's bad-mouth them. In a shrinking world, maybe we are looking at the wrong areas. Remember the four quadrant diagram first introduced in chapter 8 and shown again below?

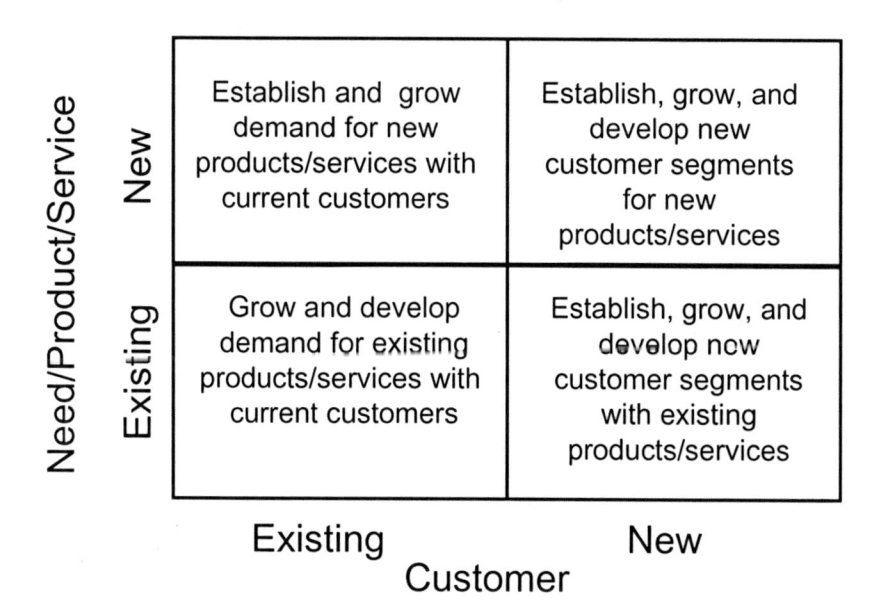

	Existing Customer	New Customer
New Need/Product/Service	Establish and grow demand for new products/services with current customers	Establish, grow, and develop new customer segments for new products/services
Existing Need/Product/Service	Grow and develop demand for existing products/services with current customers	Establish, grow, and develop new customer segments with existing products/services

Figure 13.1. The Growth Quadrant: Where Growth Happens

99

We should all be trying to create new markets. We should be trying to find our green elephant so we can help it soar to out-of-this-world success, or at least into all four quadrants. The Blue Ocean strategy tells us to make our competitors irrelevant, and I agree. How can we innovate if we are playing catch-up? Innovation requires the What, How, Why Balance, and obsessing with a competitor is totally unbalanced.

Think about different ways your current solutions, products, technologies, and services can be used by your customers. Think about your noncustomers as well. For example, imagine that you are trying to sell a luxury yacht. How many recent Ferrari or private aircraft owners have you met with lately? Think about those popular noise-reduction headsets we all wear while sitting on aircraft these days. What other use is there for that type of technology? Please, somebody invent a way to silence cell phones so the very important person next to me can shout to his heart's content down his Bluetooth and I can't hear him.

You could try to use Six Sigma tools and methods to help this creative process. Host a Growth-shop, conduct a blitz, and lead a growth diagnosis. A growth diagnosis can help establish where the gaps are in the marketplace. Another effective tool is to conduct a DOE (design of experiments) on your competitors. A DOE is a method that allows you to test alternative outcomes of an event by changing various inputs. See what happens when you focus on the market and needs/desires of the customer versus concentrating on your prime competitor. Develop creative solutions to fill the gaps in the market, like Southwest Airlines and Cirque du Soleil did.

While we focus on our competition, we are leaving less time to be creative, less time to turn dreams into reality. We can't ignore our major competitors, as we all have to make our numbers every month, but to grow, we need to be more creative and connect the dots between complementing technologies and products and services. In essence, our competition should be irrelevant. Think again of how Southwest turned the air passenger industry upside down by ignoring the traditional hub-and-spoke design and introducing point-to-point service. Southwest offered an alternative not only to air passengers, but to drivers as well. Also, think about how Starbucks created an experience for their customers rather than focusing on coffee. Look at how the iPod personifies cool. Dozens of mp3 players flood the market, but iPod is the cool one that everybody wears (as evidenced by the number of people you see walking around with those highly recognizable white ear buds!). Think about Dell and how they introduced a new business model through their organizational Innovation. All these examples exhibit the What, How, Why Balance.

Making the competition irrelevant means that they are always playing catch-up, not you. You create a new game and a new standard. Your automobile will make the buggy whip irrelevant. You set the expectations and the pricing, and the competition has to offer a better price to replace you in the new market you just created.

Ask yourself: are you currently obsessed with a competitor? Do you want to be like them? Stop it! You will never be like them. If you are obsessing, it must be because they are better than you or they make more money or they are lucky. Luck is merely where opportunity meets preparedness. So are you prepared? Are you ready to be lucky? Now there's a notion—a lucky competitor! Could that be a vital lie?

Being obsessed by the wrong thing, such as a competitor, can be dangerous. There is a cute story I first read when it was doing the joke rounds on email in 2006. The story, which I am paraphrasing, is about a vampire bat called Vinnie. Poor old Vinnie was jealous of Lucy because she always seemed able to feast on her favorite food. One morning, after a long night, the bat clan was amazed to see Vinnie arrive back at the cave covered in blood. Naturally they were curious and asked where he had been. Vinnie was tired and ignored them, but they wouldn't let him rest. They again asked where he had been and how he had managed to end up covered in blood. Realizing that he would not be able to rest until he explained, Vinnie eventually beckoned his fellow bats to follow him. Along the way he explained how he had followed Lucy. He pointed out several landmarks and remarked at how beautiful everything was. The bats had to agree. He explained how he continued to follow Lucy as she flew by churches and manor houses and across the cemetery. After a while he pointed to a tree. "Do you see that tree, the beautiful oak tree?" "Yes" was the unanimous response. "Well, I didn't. Now leave me alone!" Don't be like Vinnie; don't aimlessly follow your competitors. You will more than likely end up with a bloody nose.

Try thinking about some of the issues facing the world today—for example, the job drain to India and China. Couple that with another macro economic fact—for example, there are approximately eight hundred billionaires in the world. How many are in India? How many in China? I can tell you that there are probably more than you think and even more in Russia. What opportunity does that give you? Is there some way to break into those markets before your competition? How about creating new markets in those areas?

What about the U.S. and European billionaires? What are billionaires buying today? Today's luxury goods may be ripe for massive worldwide commercialization in the future. Can you be the first to market with a voice-cancellation system to silence annoying cell calls in your vicinity? What else could this type of technology be used for? What other cool things could take the market by storm? What about a machine that exercises you while you sleep? A zero-calorie, great-tasting beer would be nice, too!

Making your competition irrelevant doesn't need to be through high technology or finding a new marketplace in outer Timbuktu. If you are relentless in finding ways to make your customers successful, they may prefer to remain loyal to you. Loyalty is a way of making your competition irrelevant, too. Think again of Southwest Airlines and how they have loyal customers because the company makes it easy to travel with them. Think how Starbucks' customers are loyal because of the atmosphere and experience of drinking in the company's coffee shops. Think how McDonald's got their loyalty by thinking way beyond the taste of the burger.

Be balanced in your approach, and make sure you meet the minimum threshold in your intellectual, organizational, and human elements. Obsession with a competitor will almost certainly lead to unbalanced Innovation. Moving to those out-of-this-world success levels by making your competitors irrelevant will require a balanced approach to Innovation. Strategic use of Six Sigma can help bring together the ideas, energy, and passions of the human, intellectual, and organizational factors to ensure that Innovation is balanced. Balanced Innovation will create growth.

Focus on the What, How, Why Balance, and let your competitors focus on you.

Key Points in Chapter 13

- » Innovation requires the right What, How, Why Balance.
- » Obsessing about your competition is not good for your health.
- » Being obsessed with a competitor is unbalanced.
- » Use Six Sigma tools like DOE to understand how you react to your customers and competitors.
- » Conduct a workshop to discover where the gaps are in the market.
- » Develop solutions aimed at exploiting the gaps.
- » Make your competition play catch-up, not yourself.
- » Take advantage of the shrinking world.
- » Luck is where opportunity meets preparedness; be prepared.
- » Focus on the What, How, Why Balance, and let your competitors focus on you.

Key Questions to Ask Yourself

- » Are you currently obsessed about one or more of your competitors?
- » What can you do to make your competition irrelevant?
- » How can you create an environment that allows you to focus on your customer and not the competition to permit and fuel Balanced Innovation?
- » How loyal is your customer base? Why? What can you do to improve customer loyalty?
- » Are you ready to be lucky?

chapter 14

hurdle the barrier

Painkillers and Banks

Even Balanced Innovation encounters barriers. Here are some suggestions for how to overcome them.

Wherever we go in life, whatever our personal and career goals, we will always encounter barriers. If you really want to validate the What, How, Why Balance of Innovation, you will need to hurdle barriers. A barrier is often caused by well-meaning intentions. It is very often the result of a vital lie or limiting assumption. "We don't have the budget for that." "The boss will never accept that." "It's too risky." "No because."

I'm sure you hear this kind of thing everyday. Sometimes the barrier is real and your discretionary budgets are overstretched, the boss has her own favorite projects, or there is a tangible risk. Remember that discretionary budgets are monies that are set aside for investments, such as research and development. Discretionary budgets are used at the discretion of leadership. Another cause of a barrier could be a constraint.[1] A constraint is otherwise known as a bottleneck, or the slowest part of a process. The constraint can be internal or external (market driven).

The barrier is usually a symptom and not a cause. It is important to attack the root cause. For example, a driver may be experiencing reduced fuel efficiency in her car. One solution could be to drive with a lighter right foot, another may be to drive shorter distances, and

1   Eliyahu Goldratt, *The Theory of Constraints*

another could be to simply increase the budget for travel. But what if the efficiency was down because a leaky gasket was causing more oil to get into the fuel system? If the root cause is not found, the fuel consumption will probably continue to reduce. All of a sudden on a cold, rainy night in the middle of nowhere, the engine blows. This is akin to papering over the cracks in a wall without finding out why the cracks have suddenly appeared. Or taking a painkiller to get rid of a headache without trying to find out what caused the headache in the first place. Taking the pill may enable you to function for a while, but if you don't find the root cause, your headache will likely return.

In a business context, the barrier to growth may be a slowing down of customer orders. This could be for a variety of reasons, and some creative thought will be required to overcome the problem. Bennett Neiman, author of *Slay the Dragons, Free the Genie,* tells the story of a branch of Citibank. Every Friday was payday, and folks would religiously trudge off to the bank to join the long lines of people waiting to cash their checks. Customers were getting more frustrated every Friday and started to look for alternatives to the banks. During one thought-provoking brainstorming session, a bank clerk said, "What if we could know in advance what each customer wanted, and then have the exact amount ready before the midday rush?" A colleague added, "Yes, and what if we could find a way to have that money in a box? The customer could put in the check and take out the money to the value of the check." A third colleague chimed in. "Yes, and what if we could find a way to only give money out to the exact amount of the request via an automatic process?" The brainstorming continued, and, according to Bennet Neiman, a few months later the bank introduced an automatic teller machine (ATM). This method of brainstorming is known as the thought association method.

Barriers can cause organizations to become introspective. They force behaviors that create unbalanced Innovation because people revert to what they do best at the expense of what may be most important. Don't let barriers go undetected and untreated. Hurdle the barrier so that your Innovation remains balanced.

Once the cause of the barrier or constraint has been established, it is time to understand what opportunities there are to overcome them. Then you can develop solutions and action plans. The process is simple:

- » Understand the environment and/or business need.
- » Understand the symptoms of the problems.
- » Drill down to the root cause of the problem.
- » Validate that you have found the root cause.
- » Develop opportunities to overcome the root causes around the symptoms that will have most impact on overcoming the barriers and constraints.
- » Develop solutions and action plans.
- » Execute (using the 5-D process).

Many great tools exist to help find root causes and you can find a brief explanation of some of these tools in Appendix A. For example, check out the fishbone diagram, reality trees, and other causal analysis tools. A simple tool such as 5-Whys can be quick and effective. Simply put, 5-Whys is when you ask a series of questions beginning with *why* and culminating when you believe you have the root to the issue. Six Sigma Black Belts can be useful here, as they are trained in the use of such tools to find the root cause of a problem. Try using a root-cause analysis to develop opportunities as well.

Personas and Making Wild Wishes

In addition to the thought association method used in the bank example above, I have found two other fun, rewarding methods to use during brainstorming sessions. The first is to take on the persona of somebody else. For example, if the team is stuck, ask each member to pretend to be somebody else. At first this could be somebody famous, such as pop singer Madonna or comedy actor Jim Carrey. Jim Carrey would no doubt solve a problem in a very different way than a program manager would. After a few minutes of fun, you will need to bring the team back into focus. Initially you could ask how an entrepreneur like Bill Gates would solve the problem, or Walt Disney, Winston Churchill, or even your own CEO. The first part of this method creates wild freethinking; the second part brings the session back to the problem at hand. The persona method is also a very powerful tool!

Another method is called a wild wish fantasy. The following story also comes from Bennett Neimans' book, *Slay the Dragons, Free the Genie*. Four men worked all winter in the Colorado Rockies for the power company. They had dangerous jobs, but with the danger didn't come the usual excitement; it was boring as hell. These men were responsible for keeping the power lines clear of snow and ice. Their method was to climb up the tall cable pylons dotted all over the country. When they reached a certain height, they would simply bash the cables with a long fiberglass pole.

One night as they were thawing out over a cup of hot chocolate (yeah, right), one of the guys mentioned that on his way to the mountains the previous week, he saw a squirrel clamber across a telephone cable, brushing the snow away with his tail. "What we need is a bunch of squirrels," he told his colleagues. After a few moments, one of the others added, "Squirrels aren't big enough. What we need is a bear." "A bear! Are you nuts? How will we get a bear up there?" Again, a few moments passed and refills of the miraculous hot chocolate were doled out. "Bears like honey. What we should do is put a huge honey pot at the top of the pylons." "How will we get a huge honey pot on top of the pylons to entice the bears?" Again, more hot chocolate. "What if we hired a helicopter to fly over the pylons and lower the honey pots? We can be there and fix it firmly to the pylon."

Before trying the honey pot approach, the men realized that the thrust from the helicopters would probably be incredibly powerful. The power company agreed and they were right, the thrust from the rotor on the first helicopter was so powerful that it knocked all the snow off the power lines. To this day, the power company uses helicopters to clear snow and ice off their cables.

We could use this thought process to develop a solution to silence the cell phone users in the wild wish I mentioned earlier.

"I'm tired of listening to folks yelling down telephones as soon as I land at an airport. We need thought-transfer communication." "Yeah right, beam me up! That technology doesn't exist." "No, but noise-canceling headphone technology does. Can we utilize that?"

"Maybe, but we would need to reverse the process—allow noise but kill discrete voice sounds." "I wonder if we could do that with current microphone technology in a dynamic environment." "Probably not—we would need people to wear some kind of a mask. We need to do it without masks." "What if the aircraft cabin had some discretely positioned voice-canceling transmitters above every seat?"

I'm sure you get the idea. I don't know if the business case is there, but imagine the stress relief it would provide. The telephone user could hold a more private conversation as well. This might just work in an office as well. Imagine this technology in a luxury car that allows music and conversation but reduces wind, engine, and road noises. Think how much weight we could save by using this technique instead of soundproofing. This in turn could lead to fuel efficiencies and a decrease in the reliance on fossil fuels. It could help hybrid cars become more attractive because of improved performance. Why stop at a luxury car? Perhaps by 2020 every car in the world will have noise-reduction technology. You heard it here first, folks. If anybody wants to design the system and apply for a patent, I'm sure we can strike a deal! Try to solve one of your problems by using one of these brainstorming techniques.

Brainstorming

Successful brainstorming requires good questions to get your minds thinking in the right way. To overcome barriers, I regularly use questions such as "I wish I knew how to" or "how can we." To help you find root causes, a good question to ask is "Why?" For example, "Why can't we get the vice president to release funds to do this?" The immediate answer could be, "Because we are overspent on our discretionary budget." Eventually we may find that we are spending money in the wrong places, or that the discretionary budget this year is low due to a lower return on profits last year. Another reason could be that the stock price is low and nobody is prepared to take a risk on a new venture. The "how can we" type of question could then be, "How can we fund this project by using other people's money (i.e., not our own discretionary funds)?"

This organizational or commercial Innovation coupled with intellectual Innovation can be very powerful. When you add in human factors like emotions, the ideas and passions are suddenly turbocharged with energy. Six Sigma methods, techniques, and tools are excellent in enabling this type of Innovation by providing the data and information to make knowledge-based decisions.

Any good brainstorming session will be well facilitated. It is key to have the right people in the room and to create an atmosphere that encourages freethinking and open-ended communication. Make sure the invites go out early so you have a sporting chance that calendars will be free.

No idea is a bad idea. Once an idea gets raised, it belongs to the group. Ask the team to check egos at the door and start with a good icebreaker. If some team members don't know each other, you could start by getting everybody to stand up and shake hands with the people they don't know while introducing themselves. After the formal introductions, ask group members to share something they are passionate about that is outside the working environment. There are always a few people who instantly connect at this point. Another good icebreaker is to ask each team member to tell a fact and fiction about themselves and let the group guess which is which. Icebreakers really help set the scene and get a positive emotion running through the group.

Many techniques will ensure that all voices are heard, but here are a couple of my favorites. Try rapid-fire brainstorming, where everybody writes their ideas quickly on sticky notes. Ask the group to put one idea per note, and ask that each idea include both a noun and a verb. When the idea generation slows down, look at all the ideas and group them. The themes and patterns will reveal areas you need to concentrate on.

Another of my favorites is the "yes and" approach. In small groups, get one person to start with an idea. For example, "What if we added a chocolate coating to our health bar?" The next person might say, "Yes, and we could also make it jumbo sized." The third person could say, "Yes, and we could include a chance to win a prize on certain wrappers." This continues until all members of the group have had a turn.

By having the right mix of subject matter experts (SMEs) in the team, you get early buy-in and more meaningful results. Try to get a mix of right- and left-brainers. If appropriate, bring in an outsider to help. If appropriate, ask a child or teenager; they always look at the world from a different viewpoint. That different viewpoint could be the catalyst for a brilliant new idea.

Hurdling barriers is essential in validating the What, How, Why Balance of the intellectual, organizational, and human factors of Innovation. Don't let barriers stall or prevent Innovation.

Key Points in Chapter 14

- » Barriers are usually the symptom, not the cause.
- » Barriers force behaviors that create unbalanced Innovation.
- » Hurdle the barrier by finding the root cause, establishing opportunities, and then executing developed solutions.
- » Use creative brainstorming techniques.
- » Successful brainstorming is dependent on asking the right questions.
- » Get help from SMEs and Six Sigma Black Belts when you need it.
- » Ask a young person how he or she would solve the problem.
- » Don't let a barrier prevent Balanced Innovation.

Key Questions to Ask Yourself

- » How can you create an environment that allows free thought so you can hurdle the barrier?
- » What are the constraints keeping you back? Why are they in place? What can you do about them?
- » Is your work fun?
- » What bugs you that you should hurdle and leave behind?
- » How will you start to ask the "how can we" and "I wish I knew how to" questions?
- » What areas of concern do you have that the "how can we" and "I wish I knew how to" questions could help?
- » When are you going to try asking, "How can we," or "I wish I knew how to."

chapter 15

developing your what, how, why balance

A personal development program will reap major benefits as you strive toward your own personal What, How, Why Balance. Focus on developing your knowledge, skills, expertise, and ultimately, your wisdom. Send yourself and your coworkers to look at how companies outside your industry do business. How do they train? What learning objectives do they have? Invite the organization you are benchmarking with to your learning and training classes. Treat every day as an opportunity to learn something new. It is so important to continue to challenge yourself with new learning. Remember to share what you learn and what you experience.

Most businesspeople I know spend way too much time on airplanes, flying across the world. Don't think that this is wasted time, even though until airborne connectivity becomes the norm, many of you always will. But the quiet time on an airplane ride is a golden opportunity for you to learn.

Try reading three different books every month. I like to read a variety of books, such as a new book about business trends, a pure fiction book to let my mind wander off into another world, and a classic work of literature. If you haven't read a classic for a while, try to introduce yourself to something by Dickens, Twain, Conan Doyle, the Brontë sisters, or Hemingway. These books are so rich that you can't help but get a spiritual lift from reading them. If you struggle to read, get books on CD or download mp3 versions onto your iPod or other portable device.

Try new things as you read the business books. Find the relevance between the writing and your current projects. How can you use the ideas to enable success in your business or home life? How will you use what you read in this book? How will you become more balanced and reach levels of success so far not even dreamed about? Buy a copy of the *Balanced Innovator* for all your friends, colleagues, and other associates. Collectively work on your What, How, Why Balance.

Take training classes, as many as your organization and your time will allow. Volunteer to teach students in your given subject. It's amazing how fulfilling it can be to help others develop. Try to coach and mentor as many people as you can, every week of every year. My greatest pleasure is when people I am coaching accomplish great things. One day you might be working for some of the people you have mentored, and they will remember the positive coaching they received from you. This is a behavior we should all aspire to because it really is infectious.

Take control of your own development, but work hard at helping others develop and take control of their own careers. There is great reward in seeing somebody you are coaching get promoted or achieve something special.

Any organization needs to develop their people; a people development program that trains, coaches, and mentors staff is a key tool in achieving this worthy goal. Six Sigma is a strategic imperative, and training Black Belts and Green Belts for future leadership positions should be part of the people development strategy.

Key Points in Chapter 15

- » Develop your personal What, How, Why Balance.
- » People development is key to organizational success.
- » Take control of your own personal development.
- » Read as often as you can.
- » Help develop others; it is very rewarding.

Key Questions to Ask Yourself

- » What books have you meant to read but never got around to?
- » How often do you look through a trade magazine, *The Economist,* or *Business Week* to stay current?
- » Do you know how companies outside your industry stay contemporary?
- » How many training courses have you attended in the last three years? What did you learn? What did you share?
- » Have you used vital lies to justify missing a training course?
- » What new tools and techniques have you tried recently?

chapter 16

some thoughts on leadership

Create the Right Environment

The most important thing a leader can do is create an environment that enables the team to excel. Everything else is cream. A Great leader allows the team to explore the realms of the possible. That doesn't mean that leaders abandon their teams; it means they provide support and resource as necessary, but they don't get in the way. Great leaders understand the importance of balance in everything they do. Every great leader throughout history balanced their intellectual, organizational, and human factors (see the preface for some great examples). Great leaders understand that Innovation has to add value in some way, and they understand that balanced Innovation leads to growth. A Great leader will develop a team with the right What, How, Why Balance.

Great leaders recognize that they don't have all the answers. Great leaders will take as much help as they can get. Great leaders surround themselves with people who will help them be successful. Great leaders focus on the success of their team members, individually and collectively. They have a balanced team because a balanced team is needed for balanced Innovation. A Six Sigma Black Belt provides the kind of help that leaders need to enable balance.

Terri Sjodin, motivational speaker and author of *New Sales Speak*, likes to tell a story of her first meeting with Olympic gold-medal gymnast Mitch Gaylord. During the meeting she asked, "What is it like to score a Perfect 10 at the Olympics?" Mitch replied, "You know, when you get to the final stage of a competition as big as the

Olympics, everybody left in is capable of the Perfect 10. It's all about who brings it to the contest on that day." Six Sigma Black Belts help their leaders to achieve that Perfect 10 on a consistent basis.

Form partnerships between your leaders and Black Belts. If Six Sigma is a strategic imperative, the Six Sigma Black Belts and Master Black Belts must step up and become valued members of the leadership team. Get more right-brainers into Six Sigma. Have the leader and Black Belt share goals and match their rewards so that the Black Belt is focused on the success of the leader who is rewarded in line with the success of the organization.

Passion

Throughout this book, we have talked about passion. Nothing is ever achieved without passion. It is the most important aspect of success. Without passion, everything you do becomes a chore. Your desire determines your destiny. Think of great leaders, and you will be struck by their passion: Gandhi for human rights, Winston Churchill for freedom, Martin Luther King Jr. for equality, Bill Gates for technology. Anyone who lives beyond an ordinary life has great desire. It's true in any field: weak desire brings weak results, just as a small fire creates little heat. The stronger the fire, the greater the desire will be and the greater the potential for success. Passion is the first step on the way to achievement.

Think about the great leaders you have met or worked for. How much passion did they have for their work? Think about the jobs and projects you have been involved in. Remember the ones you had a passion for. Weren't they so much more fun, and didn't you achieve so much more and get so much more out of them?

Choose the Six Sigma projects of your team where there is passion for the subject matter. A Six Sigma project with full commitment and passion will yield tremendous rewards.

Attitude

Equally important is your attitude. Your attitude is reflected in your behavior, and no matter how high your values are, it is your behavior by which you are judged. On your worst days, have a great attitude; at all other times, make sure your attitude is excellent.

This is important everywhere and in everything we do. An editorial in the April 17, 2006 *USA Today* talked about the behavior of CEOs and being nice to waiters. The article stated that a person who is nice to you but rude to a waiter is not a nice person. I suggest that you go further than this. I try to follow this simple rule that I first heard on an Earl Nightingale tape, an abridged version of his book *Lead the Field*: "Treat every person you meet as though they are the most important person in the world, because they are—to somebody!"

Lifestyle

Leaders need to be fit and healthy. Incredible pressure today can put us under terrible stress, and our performance suffers if we are unhealthy or unfit. It becomes a vicious circle as this produces more pressure, leading to worse health, a further decrease in performance, and so on.

Drink less alcohol, exercise, and try to sleep better. Park your car further away from your destination and walk the extra quarter mile. If you do this twice a day, you'll walk an extra mile each day. When you need to visit a bathroom, don't go to the one near your office; walk to one a couple of hundred yards away. Eight visits a day means an extra two miles walked. And take a pad and pencil with you or a voice recorder. It's amazing how walking can free your mind. You will want to capture those thoughts as you walk.

Bluetooth technology allows us to communicate while mobile. Try to make the next conference call while moving around, at least while you don't need to be staring at a computer screen. At the airport, try to walk between flights, even if it means going to a new terminal. Getting the train between two terminals has two negative effects: you are missing out on the opportunity to exercise, and you are exposing yourself to another enclosed, germ-ridden environment.

Travelers struggle to eat well. A rich meal and a nightcap in the bar with a colleague can be tempting. Try a salad or bowl of soup instead of a steak, keep your starch levels down, and don't forget your vitamins and minerals. At breakfast have a bowl of cereal instead of a three-egg omelet, and use fat-free or soy milk.

So even if you don't have time to go to the gym, you can do simple things to ensure that your mind and body can operate at full throttle when you need them to.

Teamwork

The best leaders understand the benefits of their teams. You may have heard popular business terms such as *servant leader, leader follower,* and *benevolent leader*[1]. Each of these terms refers to the way leaders develop and encourage the people around them by setting objectives then leaving their people to use their own methods to achieve these objectives. The leaders' role is to help overcome barriers and find the right resources to help the team be successful. The leaders know that the success of their team reflects on them.

The point is to develop the people around you. Great leaders know that they don't climb to the top of the tree; they are carried there. Succession plans are great, but help your people get there. Great leaders willingly delegate both non-critical and critical tasks to subordinates. Although they delegate, they will never abandon; they will keep a watchful eye on progress and allow team members to benefit from the biggest challenges.

If you are a Six Sigma Black Belt, try a project that creates an environment to enable team members to succeed.

Great leaders are never micromanagers; they attract the best to work with them by giving them more authority. A great leader will lead, follow, and get out of the way by clearly setting expectations. In effect, great leaders sponsor their subordinates and do all they can to make them successful. They will provide the necessary resources, and they will clear roadblocks.

Using a sports analogy, it is all about the team. A great quarterback will always lose if nobody on the team can catch the ball.

Remember that a team celebrates together. An individual cele-

---

1   James Citrin and Richard Smith, *The 5 Patterns of Extraordinary Leadership*

bration, no matter how great the achievement, can be lonely. Don't forget the acronym for TEAM: Together Everyone Achieves More.

Leaders allow their subordinates the freedom to define the process to achieve objectives. They don't tell their subordinates how to get there. They are comfortable hiring people more qualified in specific areas than themselves. Once a new recruit is hired, the great leader gives them the freedom to achieve his or her potential. A great leader will borrow the brainpower of others for the greater good of the team.

Great leaders are passionate. They love the organization they work for and the customer they support. Great leaders have great attitudes. Great leaders generate positive energetic emotions. Great leaders communicate, communicate, and then communicate.

A great leader uses his or her social network and the social networks of everybody around them. They also share willingly their social networks. A great leader never criticizes in public. A great leader is confident but not arrogant. A great leader's passion is not obsession.

Great leaders are listeners. The first step to wisdom is silence, and the second step is listening—listening with empathy.

Great leaders understand that they are working for numerous people, including customers, employees, and shareholders.

Great leaders know how to make decisions under uncertainty; they will allow the data to drive information-based decisions. Great leaders can influence even when they don't have the authority.

Six Sigma Black Belts are often great leaders, and they enable their leaders, peers, and subordinates to succeed. They enable the Perfect 10.

Great leaders always try to do the right things, even when nobody is watching. It becomes a habit and sets up behaviors that they are judged by.

Be a great leader, be healthy, and use Six Sigma to help you take your personal and business life to the next level where you will create, develop, and validate your What, How, Why Balance.

Key Points in Chapter 16

- » Leaders need to create an environment that ensures team members can excel.
- » Leaders understand the impact of the What, How, Why Balance and why it leads to success.
- » Great leaders understand the importance of Innovation and how Balanced Innovation leads to growth.
- » Six Sigma Black Belts enable the success of their leaders.
- » Six Sigma Black Belts help to consistently hit the Perfect 10.
- » On your worst days, have a great attitude; at all other times, make sure your attitude is excellent.
- » Treat every person as though they are the most important person in the world
- » Great leaders have passion but are not obsessive.
- » TEAM means Together Everyone Achieves More.
- » Great leaders understand the importance of being fit and healthy.
- » Great leaders understand the importance of developing others.
- » Great leaders know that the team success is more important than the success of any individuals.
- » Great leaders delegate even the most important tasks.
- » Great leaders never forget who they are working for.
- » Great leaders are not afraid of uncertainty.
- » Great leaders learn how to influence without authority.
- » Six Sigma Black Belts enable the success of the team.
- » Develop teams with What, How, Why Balance.

Key Questions to Ask Yourself

- » What is your attitude and behavior like when you are frustrated? Does it match your values?
- » Do you treat everybody you meet with respect? How can you change to achieve this simple objective?
- » How often do you share success with your team?

- » Are you comfortable delegating important tasks? Why?
- » How can you prepare yourself to become a great leader?
- » Do you partner with your Six Sigma Black Belts to enable your success?

chapter 17

3-2-1 blastoff

I have been asked this question many times: if I could start my career over again, would I do anything different? The answer is a resounding "yes!" I would have continued to learn and improve after college and earning my executive MBA. When I achieved my MBA, I thought, *Thank God! Now I don't have to worry about that stuff ever again.* How wrong I was. Trust me, every day you should try to learn something new. Read as often as you can, and try out what thought leaders are saying.

It was my journey into Six Sigma that rekindled my thirst for knowledge. I was working with a customer in the UK who had some real challenges in terms of process control and overrunning costs. I had just received my basic Six Sigma Yellow Belt training and had a hunch that Six Sigma would really help. I was right. I took Six Sigma to the customer, and we started to see light at the end of the tunnel. We characterized the current state, found way too many UDEs and drilled down to three root causes. It was tremendously successful, and the customer loved us for it. I decided to become a Black Belt. During my training, I was introduced to dozens of new books about leadership, business, and Six Sigma. (There really are some great authors out there!)

I wanted to repeat the success we had with the UK customer with all our customers, so I quickly joined/developed a social network with a few Black Belts who were of like minds. We found several other examples of Six Sigma helping the customer, and with an almost eerie consistency, we noticed that growth followed. We spread the word and were soon getting requests for help. Six Sigma for Growth was born. Expanding to Innovation was a natural progression, and my thirst for knowledge expanded exponentially with it.

There are many reasons to use Six Sigma in a strategic way at the front end of the business. Six Sigma is all about success and quality, and it has been the catalyst for turning many organizations from inefficient dinosaurs into lean and agile business segment leaders. New business is the lifeblood of a company, yet competition grows more intense. The marketplace is dynamically evolving, with customers demanding more efficiency and effectiveness. To survive and grow, we need to be more innovative and more customer focused. To achieve this, we need to reassess how we can make our customers successful. Six Sigma can and should be a key enabler in this endeavor.

Produce an action plan. Ask yourself the key questions at the end of each of the chapters in this book. Use the 5-D process, and get help from SMEs where and when you need it. Another thing: practice! Athletes don't enter the stadium hoping to win; they practice! So should you. Practice your skills every day, and build up your strengths. Constantly assess your personal What, How, Why Balance.

Several organizations have now set up Innovation as part of their Six Sigma offerings. Some of these groups are trying to force Six Sigma tools into Innovation and rigid process into Innovation, simply because Innovation is fresh and new and something businesses should be doing They are telling you what to do and how to do it before understanding why you should do it. Make sure your Six Sigma for Innovation is balanced, and you should succeed—more importantly your Innovations should succeed, otherwise why do it? If you can't see the link and benefits, don't do it. Adding Six Sigma for Innovation seems to be the right thing to do. Enabling right-brain thinking with Six Sigma is very powerful. Try to ensure that you don't go too far into left-brain discipline though and start to overanalyze and measure, as this will stifle Innovation. It is for this reason that I developed the 5-D method—it takes away the temptation to overanalyze. Innovation happens best when the organization gets out of the way, and the informal network takes over. Six Sigma can and will enable Innovation but only when the inextricable link is understood and dreams and ideas are turned into reality by bridging the gap between the right and left hemispheres of the brain. Bridge the Innovation Gap with Six Sigma to help you propel your success.

If you are looking for a Six Sigma for Innovation program or training class, make sure your proposed mentors have a balanced approach. The human factors are just as important as the intellectual and organizational factors. If the emotional connections are not positive and strong, it is quite probable that the Why question hasn't been adequately addressed. If the focus is on the What and the How to the detriment of the Why, it is likely that you are being offered traditional Six Sigma tools force-fed into Innovation. This is obviously the wrong way around and will soon lead to dissatisfaction. Make sure you fully understand why Six Sigma can and will enable Innovation before undertaking the What and the How.

What Can We Do?

You could create an environment for Innovation like a Sigmavation Station, where intellectual and emotional thoughts can be shared to create value. This is an area where Innovation can take off. It could be a virtual environment or co-located in a war room. It should be used to encourage creativity and Innovation, to push the limits of your imagination by exploring the realms of the possible. It is a thought-space where ideas can be turned into reality. It is an environment where the human, intellectual, and organizational factors come together and Six Sigma enables the ideas, energy, and passion of these factors. It can be a growth shop, a customer blitz, a growth diagnosis, a collaboration workshop, or many other things. More details on these will appear later in this chapter. You could try to devote space on a large wall for idea generation and development. Write an idea on a wall, and encourage everybody who passes by to contribute to its development. Have others put their ideas on the wall, too. This is powerful not only in generating ideas, but in getting buy-in. It will motivate people to create more and better ideas. All ideas placed on the wall belong to the organization, not the individuals who raise them, although you may want to include some kind of reward scheme for contributors. Ask your customers and suppliers to add their ideas and thoughts, too.

A **Growth-shop** is an excellent way to reinvigorate an organization toward growth. It is a workshop aimed at realizing a series of key actions to develop a growth strategy.

A Growth-shop is usually conducted in two sessions, an evening social and a half-day workshop the following day. The evening social includes a short brainstorming session where participants are asked two questions: what are the major barriers to growth in your organization, and where are the major growth opportunities? The output from the social forms the basis for the workshop on the following day.

The objectives are to identify opportunities for and barriers to growth, to prioritize those barriers and opportunities by business/product line, and to begin developing action plans for the top priorities.

A **customer blitz** is an event to understand the current state with a particular customer and to develop a coordinated, engagement strategy for that customer. The attendees are knowledgeable individuals who have worked with or are about to work with the customer. The participants review all available data regarding the customer to develop an engagement strategy and prepare for an initial customer meeting, such as a VOC event. Pre-blitz planning is the key to a successful blitz. It is important to identify the participants and issue invitations thirty to forty-five days in advance to ensure that the right people attend.

A **growth diagnosis** is a workshop aimed at finding the root cause behind both successes and failures in growing business. A growth diagnosis is all about taking current state to desired future state by finding and eliminating undesirable effects (UDEs), barriers, and constraints, while at the same time looking to build on successful activity. A successful growth diagnosis will often lead to appropriate allocation of discretionary new business funds.

A **collaboration workshop** is an interactive workshop aimed at getting a disparate group of organizations to a common vision, strategy, and action plan. The workshop is usually conducted in three phases:

1. A current state evaluation, gained through questionnaire and interviews with organization leaders, prior to the workshop.

2. A day-and-a-half workshop held on neutral premises, with a social on the evening at the end of the first day to encourage team building.
3. A follow-on action review after one month.

Attendees should be decision makers and business leaders, including business development, program management, and contracts.

The Sigmavation Station can help achieve the Balanced Innovation illustrated in figure 17.1. It is a fun place where you share your thoughts, your heart, your guts, and your soul with passionate people who share the same goals. It is where the different SMEs gather together as a team to create more than the sum of the parts. The Sigmavation Station helps you bridge the gap between the right and left hemispheres of the brain and turn dreams into reality.

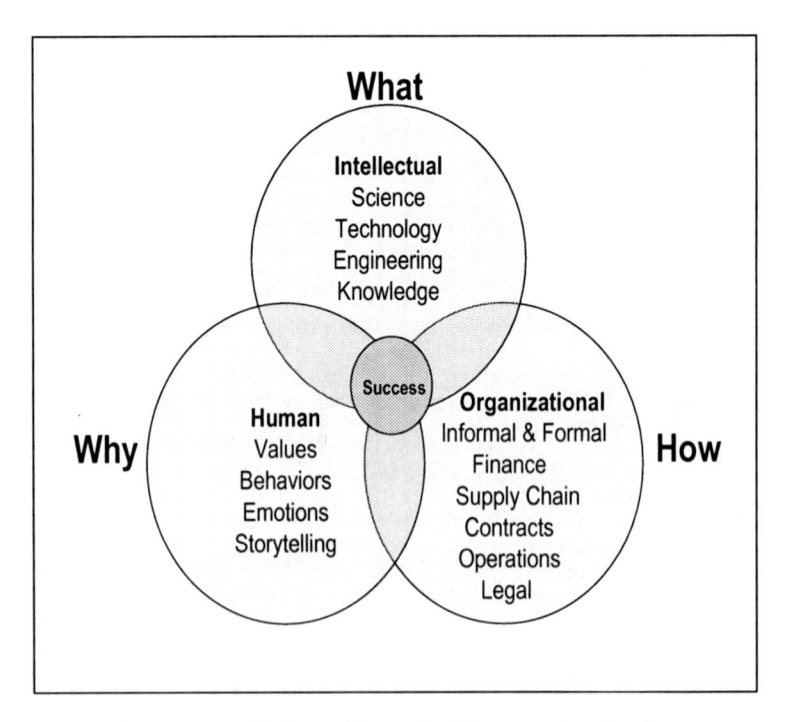

Figure 17.1. Balance from the Sigmavation Station

Why not take off to those out-of-this-world levels of success from the Sigmavation Station? The Sigmavation Station provides a balanced approach to Innovation, ensuring equal importance is placed on the human and organizational factors as is on the intellectual factors.

What Should We Do?

Use the Sigmavation Station and your Six Sigma tools and methods to help understand the current state of balance. Have you adequately addressed the organizational, human, and intellectual factors? Does each of these factors achieve a minimum threshold? Does each factor validate the others? Try using a simple tool like a stakeholder grid to understand the level of support from the key resources—internal and external—including your customers.

Any Innovation or new product development is exciting, but often they don't work and great deals of money, time, and other resources are expended. The balanced approach allows early decision making. First we have to understand the current state, which is harder than it sounds. Intuition is a very powerful tool, and an outsider might be able to assess your level of balance just by observing the dynamics of the team. But usually, intuition is often not enough to convince leaders that their team is on the wrong track or is lacking in some way.

To combat this, I have developed a method and tool called the Balance Indicator that you can also use. I work with the sponsor and the key team members and other stakeholders whom I ask a series of questions. The multiple-choice answers provide numeric inputs for each of the intellectual, organizational, and human areas of the balance model. This dictates the size of each of the three circles. The intersections between the three factors are also measured. From this you can see graphically the current state of balance. My tool shows the aggregate, the average, and any number of other scenarios to validate the balance.

More often than not, the tool verifies what intuition has already figured out, but it's amazing how leaders accept the result with facts and data. Once the current state is understood and agreed, we can drill down to the root cause of the issues and make decisions accordingly. This decision could be to kill a program that has little chance of success or to address the balance and bridge the gap. The earlier these types of decisions are made, the more chance of success.

128   the balanced innovator

Once you have a good understanding of balance, you could use a network analysis tool to help understand the strength of the relationships. Use the outer loop of the 5-D methodology to ensure you understand the market and what is bothering your key customers. Try a design of experiments (DOE) to address some "what if" questions and scenarios. When you have a good handle on the current state of your balance, you could use a Failure Modes Effects Analysis (FMEA) to assess and understands the risks. A thorough and honest assessment will likely show the reasons behind the less-than-ideal level of balance. Understand why that is. Find the undesirable effects (UDEs) that highlight the issue, and then drill down to the root causes. Once the root causes have been established, you can prepare opportunity statements and potential benefits. Understand the barriers and constraints that could stop the opportunities coming to fruition, and plan to overcome them.

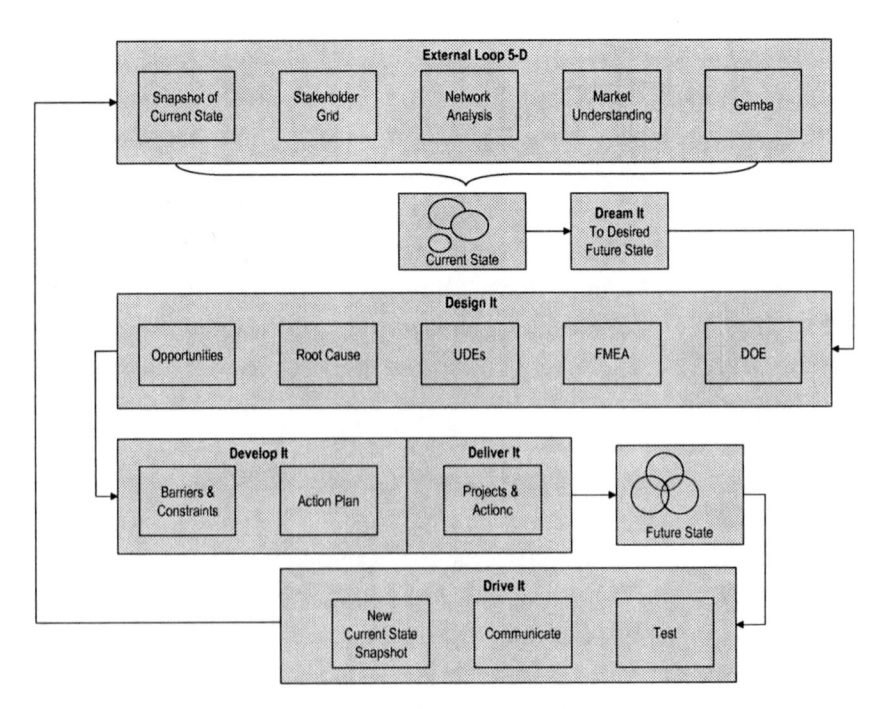

Figure 17.2 Achieving Balance

Once the action plan is in place, start to implement the projects and move from an unbalanced situation to a balanced one. As you move into the Drive It phase of the 5-D methodology, test your results with something like a peer review or a pilot project. Make sure you communicate progress with all stakeholders. The communication and storytelling fully validates the strong intellectual, organizational, and human factors. Figure 17.2 shows this simple step-by-step approach, which can help bridge the gap between the unbalanced, original current state and the desired and balanced future state—in other words, to help you to bridge the Innovation Gap.

My intent in writing this book is to provide an entertaining and hopefully inspiring way of sharing how Six Sigma can enable profitable business growth and Innovation. I also wanted to provide a set of practical examples and useful tools to help you on this exciting journey. Nobody has all the answers, particularly in terms of business growth and Innovation, but what I have provided is a means to help you connect the dots, discover how to hunt for opportunities, and help you understand both the art and science of Innovation and growth. You should now be in a very good position to develop the right What, How, Why Balance.

How many people read a business book, take a few notes, try the new ideas for a couple of weeks, and then add the book to the other dust collectors on the office shelf? Don't just read this book. Study it, underline the points that you feel are most relevant to you, highlight them, answer the questions raised, and take your organization to the next level.

I hope that this book has been useful to you. I hope that you are now ready to take off. I don't expect you to agree with everything you have read. In fact, I want you to challenge my ideas in a positive way that makes your success personal to you and moves both your career and business into overdrive. Spread the word, and take others with you. It will be challenging, it should be rewarding, and it will be fun.

Key Points in Chapter 17

- » Ensure that you are balanced between the intellectual, organizational, and human factors in everything you do.
- » Six Sigma can enable business growth.
- » Six Sigma can enable Innovation.
- » Develop a Sigmavation Station.
- » Develop your What, How, Why Balance.

Key Questions to Ask

- » What are you waiting for?

chapter 18

conclusion

The primary aim of this book is to help organizations become better at Innovation. To do this requires an understanding of the balance between the intellectual, organizational, and human factors that turn creative ideas into reality. Said another way, balancing What we do, know, and offer; How we learn, share, and organize; and Why we do those things helps us turn dreams into reality. The Why validates the What and How, and vice versa.

Some of this book encourages the reader to consider using the methods of Six Sigma to enable Innovation. I was first trained in Six Sigma in 2003 and became a Black Belt in 2004. With a strong background in business development, I was fascinated by two things: first how to use Six Sigma to enable Innovation and revenue growth and second why nobody else seemed to be doing it. Organizations such as GE, Honeywell, Bank of America, Raytheon, and Motorola have had tremendous success with Six Sigma. The strategic needs of the first pioneers of Six Sigma, such as Motorola and GE, were clear. They needed a methodology for quality improvement, and applying the methods across their corporations, from top to bottom and East to West, proved to be incredibly powerful. Six Sigma was about reducing risk, eliminating defects, lowering costs, and so on.

Despite the success of these and other organizations, the trend is to turn away from Six Sigma because some commentators are claiming that it stifles Innovation. Indeed, Innovation is the new big thing. If we are now moving away from risk-averse, belt-tightening strategies to more risk-taking Innovation, why can't Six Sigma be used to manage the risk? Tools like FMEA (Failure Modes Effects Analysis) are very effective and simple to use. Six Sigma professionals have an arsenal of easy-to-use tools, many of which can help innovators.

The new sport of Six Sigma bashing is almost as fashionable as Innovation in today's business publications, but is this fair? Are the writers in *Business Week* and other highly respected journals on to something? Are they reflecting the mood of our leading organizations? Are these organizations looking for a new magical formula to replace Six Sigma?

Often we move from one methodology to another for all the wrong reasons, without understanding why. So why on earth should we dump the most successful management aid of the last twenty years? Success in anything we do rarely happens by chance; it happens when we have a balance between the What, How, and Why.

Six Sigma programs that are failing or becoming stale are in trouble because this balance is missing. This is true in everything we do—from our relationships, our studies and learning, our parenting, our careers, and in the organizations we work for or belong to. It is also true with Innovation. Innovation often starts because of a passion, but if that passion is not shared, then who cares? If you are not organized in a way that helps you make the right emotional connections, or you don't tell the right story in a compelling way through your communication and behavior, is it going to be successful? Is it still Innovation, or is it now a hobby? I believe it is doomed to fail. Some people go train spotting for a hobby, others collect stamps; I don't do either of these things because they are of little or no interest to me. I know what stamp collecting is, I utmost respect the diligence and passion of stamp collectors, and I generally know how to do it, but there is no reason why I want to spend my time as a philatelist. Innovations that are based on hobbies or personal agendas are also of no interest to me. Why? I am not connected emotionally, and therefore I don't get it!

I am, as you have observed, very passionate about Innovation, and I am passionate about Six Sigma. Innovation is the introduction of something new that adds value. Six Sigma is the improvement of something that adds value. Both bridge the gap between the current state and desired future state—one by developing opportunities, the other by solving problems.

Some writers and thought leaders today believe that Six Sigma kills Innovation because of the heavy logic and analysis that accompany the measure and analyze phases of the DMAIC Six Sigma method. This, of course, would be true if the Six Sigma program addressed only the How and What. If used to enable business success by addressing the strategic needs of the organization—in other words, the Why—Six Sigma is both impressive and effective. I have seen success in this arena time and time again by adapting the Six Sigma methodology to suit the changing needs.

In *The Theory of Evolution,* Charles Darwin famously said, "It is not the strongest of the species that survives, nor the most intelligent, but the one most responsive to change." More recently, General Eric Shinseki of the U.S. Army added, "If you don't like change, you're going to like irrelevance even less." My challenge to Six Sigma professionals, organizational leaders, managers, engineers, technologists, scientists, innovators, and inventors, students, and professors is this: consider change as a friend that helps meet both the new and evolving needs of the environment we live in.

If Innovation is high on the organization's strategic agenda, then Six Sigma can enable it. They can enable each other. Six Sigma and Innovation are both needed if an organization is to stay ahead of the game by improving and growing, but only if the What, the How and the Why have the right balance. Irrelevance is not a strategic option; developing the right What, How, Why Balance is!

chapter 19

recommended further reading

Beckwith, Harry, *Selling the Invisible: A Field Guide to Modern Marketing*

Beckwith shares many great examples of how to go the extra mile in terms of service. The author helps the reader think differently about service and what customers expect.

Blanchard, Ken, and Sheldon Bowles, *Raving Fans: A Revolutionary Approach to Customer Service*

The authors provide a simple but commonsense approach to customer service. Written as an easy-to-read parable, the story revolves around a golfer and his fairy godmother who guides him through several encounters with outstanding service in a variety of business settings.

Blanchard, Ken, *Leadership Smarts: Inspiration and Wisdom from the Heart of a Leader*

Leadership Smarts contains approximately one hundred easy to understand quotes with a brief explanation of how to apply each one in everyday life. This book is a quick read that can be finished on even the shortest of plane rides.

Charan, Ram, *What the CEO Wants You to Know*

Charan captures the essence of what is important when running a business. He does this by cross-referencing his family's street merchant businesses in India during his formative years.

Charan, Ram, *Profitable Growth is Everyone's Business: 10 Tools You Can Use Monday Morning*

This book presents ten easy-to-understand ideas that the author claims the reader can start implementing the day after they are read. Don't expect anything profound, but it is an easy read with some good thoughts.

Citrin, James, and Richard Smith, *The Five Patterns of Extraordinary Careers: The Guide for Achieving Success and Satisfaction*

The five patterns referenced in this book's title include Understanding the Value of You, Practice Benevolent Leadership, Overcome the Permission Paradox, Differentiating Using the 20/80 Principle of Performance, and Find the Right Fit. As an added bonus, these authors refer the reader to a Web site that allows the reader to take a test to evaluate their personal performance within the five patterns.

Connellan, Tom, *Inside the Magic Kingdom: Seven Keys to Disney's Success*

Connellan writes a nice parable about four executives who visit Disney World in Florida to find the secret of the parks' success. Their Disney Guide introduces them to seven keys that can be used to assist success.

Covey, Stephen R., *The 7 Habits of Highly Effective People*

If you don't already know about this book, where have you been? My favorite habit is the fifth. It states, "Seek first to understand, then be understood." Covey includes several personal stories that bring the book to life.

Covey, Stephen R., *The 8th Habit: From Effectiveness to Greatness*

Almost twenty years after the first 7 habits, Covey introduces the eighth. It's about finding your voice and adds nicely to the original.

Friedman, Thomas, *The World Is Flat: A Brief History of the Twenty-first Century*

The author doesn't really think the world is flat, but he does shed tremendous insight on how it is shrinking through globalization and new technologies such as the Internet. This book includes great stories about India and China. One of its most interesting revelations involves the fact that these countries are now graduating approximately ten times more engineers each year than the United States.

Godin, Seth, *Purple Cow*

The goal of *Purple Cow* is to teach people to seek out and find things that are remarkable. The title parable is based on how boring cows are because they are common and there are millions of them. A purple cow! Now that would be remarkable.

Goldratt, Eliyahu, *The Goal*

The Goal is a parable about a struggling manufacturing company that has been focusing on efficiencies without really understanding the underlying problems within their manufacturing plant. Enter Jonah, a former professor of the plant's general manager. Jonah reminds his student that he should be finding the bottlenecks and constraints if he wants to increase productivity at the plant. Of course, there is a happy ending.

Harry, Mikel, and Richard Schroeder, *Six Sigma: The Breakthrough Management Strategy Revolutionizing the World's Top Corporations*

This book introduced the world to the DMAIC (Define, Measure, Analyze, Improve, and Control) method of Six Sigma problem solving.

Hutson, Harry, and Barbara Perry, *Putting Hope to Work*

The authors argue very nicely that optimistic companies are better at Innovation than pessimistic ones.

Johansson, Frans, *The Medici Effect: What Elephants and Epidemics can Teach us About Innovation*

The Medici Effect focuses on finding the intersection of various ideas that, when brought together, produce something special. The author illustrates his thoughts with many interesting examples.

Kim, Chan W., and Renée Mauborgne, *Blue Ocean Strategy: How to Create Uncontested Market Space and Make Competition Irrelevant*

The main concept of this book is that organizations should be focusing on creating new value rather than continually obsessing about competitors. The title comes from the idea that organizations should seek new oceans to swim in, rather than fighting for scraps in the bloody red ocean of competition.

Maxwell, John C., *Running with the Giants: What the Old Testament Heroes Want You to Know About Life and Leadership*

This book provides Maxwell's view of what some of the greatest leaders in the Bible would advise, if you were privileged enough to have a conversation with them.

McCarty, Tom, Lorraine Daniels, Michael Bremer, and Praveen Gupta, *The Six Sigma Black Belt Handbook*

This book is recommended only as a reference guide for Six Sigma practitioners or people about to introduce continuous improvement to their organization.

Nightingale, Earl, *Lead the Field*

Earl Nightingale is one of the fathers of motivation and *Lead the Field* contains several worthy nuggets of information for the would-be leader and entrepreneur.

Perkins, Dennis, *Leading at the Edge: Leadership Lessons from the Extraordinary Saga of Shackleton's Antarctic Expedition*

Perkins uses a very novel approach to get his message across by reliving the leadership skills of Ernest Shackleton's nautical adventure to the South Pole.

Pink, Daniel, *A Whole New Mind: Why Right-Brainers Will Rule the Future*

Pink argues in *A Whole New Mind* that the future belongs to the creative right-brain thinkers. This is a good thing for the traditional industrial powerhouses of the West because most left-brain jobs are, according to the author, going overseas or being automated.

Rosenfeld, Robert, *Making the Invisible Visible*

Rosenfeld covers the human side of Innovation in a completely different (but equally compelling) way than *The Balanced Innovator*. He also suggests ways in which companies can organize their Innovation efforts through the use of champions and advocates.

Sanborn, Mark, *The Fred Factor: How Passion in Your Work and Life Can Turn the Ordinary into the Extraordinary*

The Fred Factor tells a story of a postal worker named Fred. Fred delivers such great service that the author is compelled to write about the extraordinary levels of service some people seem to deliver naturally.

Sjodin, Terri, *New Sales Speak: The 9 Biggest Sales Presentation Mistakes and How to Avoid Them*

This author is also one of my favorite speakers. She discusses the nine most common mistakes people make when delivering presentations.

Stacey, Ralph D., *Strategic Management and Organizational Dynamics*

Stacey was a professor at the University of Hertfordshire when I was studying for my MBA. He has a unique view on chaos and uncertainty that more than pricked my curiosity. This book is a mix of personal views and university textbook.

Toler, Stan, *Minute Motivators for Leaders: Quick Inspiration for the Time of Your Life*

For all the same reasons I recommended Ken Blanchard's *Leadership Smarts*, I recommend this book. It is short and simple, combining great quotes with practical advice.

Warren, Rick, *The Purpose-Driven Life: What on Earth Am I Here For?*

Pastor Rick Warren explains how each of us should live a life of purpose by developing a forty-day plan that creates a personal mission statement for each of our lives. More than one hundred million readers can't be wrong. The style is easy to read, and the messages are spiritual and inspiring.

appendix a

brief description of some tools and methods

5-Whys

The 5-whys tool is a simple way to get to the root of a problem by asking "why" at each successive level of detail. It is used to explore all the possible causes of a problem or the root cause of a problem.

Affinitization

This is used to gather and group ideas. It allows a team to generate a large number of ideas through brainstorming before summarizing the ideas into groups of similar thoughts. Each group is then given a heading. It helps the team find focus amid many different ideas and opinions and can often lead to the discovery of intersections between otherwise disparate ideas.

Balance Indicator

This tool has been developed to allow leaders and decision makers to understand the current-state level of balance between the intellectual, organizational, and human factors of a project. This could be a new product development project, a new business proposal, and even something as obscure as making a career decision. Team members complete simple questionnaires. From the answers, the size of each factor and the intersections between factors are displayed.

Brainstorming

Teams use brainstorming to creatively and effectively generate a high volume of ideas on a given topic. The result of a brainstorming session is only as good as the question asked and the experience and knowledge of the team members. It is best to ask that ideas consist of both a noun and a verb to enable readers to understand the context.

Causal Analysis

This is a method used to help find the root cause of any given problem. Several tools are available such as the simple 5-whys to more sophisticated fishbone diagrams and reality trees. The outcome of a causal analysis should be a validated understanding of the real cause of a problem, not just the symptoms.

Communications Plan

A communication plan contains the details of the project and how the message is going to be shared. It should have a brief description of the vision and goals and a list of contacts that need to be informed. The plan should also include a list of all the media that will be used to get the message out. This includes e-mail, web messages, presentations, meetings, letters, trade shows, and so on.

Creative Thinking

There are several creative thinking techniques that exist. These include but are not limited to persona, wild wish fantasy, and the six thinking hats. It is important to ensure that the atmosphere and environment is conducive to creative thinking. Rules such as "all ideas are valid" and "an idea, once shared, belongs to the team" can help create the right environment.

Critical Chain

Critical Chain is the name given to the project management philosophy and methodology developed by Eli Goldratt, creator of the Theory of Constraints. It suggests the shifting of focus away from local optimization, both at the task level and the project level, to the system level. This ensures that all projects are completed on time and on budget and that they meet all requirements. This state is achieved by focusing on all the links of the project, rather than just the single critical path.

Decision Trees

Decision making is at the heart of strategy and Innovation. Making the right decision can mean the difference between success and failure. A decision tree helps leaders and decision makers make the best possible decisions when uncertainty is present. The decision tree helps assess the risks of making one decision versus another and the risks associated with making no decision.

Design of Experiments (DOE)

A Design of Experiments (DOE) is a purposeful change of inputs in order to observe corresponding changes in the output(s) of a process or event. The purpose of this is to successfully attain some objective for the output(s) by gathering as much information as possible while using as few resources as possible. This can be done to aid Innovation by looking at potential changes in the environment, such as the introduction of disruptive technology, and by assessing how a competitor might react.

Failure Modes Effects Analysis (FMEA)

This is a systematic technique to identify potential failures and prioritize the failures according to the risk in terms of severity, occurrence probability, and detection probability.

A FMEA can provide information to identify risks associated with design and process. Part of the FMEA addresses how to put actions in place that will reduce or eliminate failures.

A FMEA is about upfront planning to assure that possible failures have been considered. This minimizes the chances that these failures could occur.

Fishbone Diagram

This tool allows a team to identify, explore, and graphically display in increasing detail all the possible causes of a problem in an effort to find the root causes. The fishbone diagram looks as you might think: like a fishbone. The problem is described at the head of the fish and each main bone displays a different category such as people, materials, methods, and machinery. Subcategories are then displayed along each major category. Causes that appear repeatedly should be investigated further, as they are likely the root causes.

Force Field Analysis

A force field analysis identifies the forces and factors that support the work being undertaken versus those forces and factors that are problems and issues. It is an easy-to-use and see presentation of the positives and negatives of a situation for instant comparison.

Input Process Output (IPO)

The input-process-output formulation is perhaps the best-known aspect of systems theory. Basically, it states that a system transforms inputs into outputs via a process. It is used to analyze the various components of a system.

Listening

This is sometimes known as active listening. This is a skill as much as a tool and is used to really understand the issues of your conversational partner. Listening should be aimed at understanding before being understood (Stephen Covey's fifth habit) and should be done from the viewpoint of your partner without trying to put what they are saying into your own autobiography.

Mind Mapping

A mind map is a diagram used to represent words, ideas, tasks, or other items linked to and arranged radially around a central key word or idea. It is used to generate, visualize, structure, and classify ideas, and it is an aid in study, organization, problem solving, and decision making.

Quality Function Deployment (QFD)

QFD transforms customer needs (the voice of the customer [VOC]) into engineering characteristics (and appropriate test methods) of a product or service, prioritizing each product/service characteristic while simultaneously setting development targets for product or service development. A QFD can strongly help an organization focus on the critical characteristics of a new or existing product or service from the separate viewpoints of the customer market segments, company, or technology-development needs.

Reality Tree

Reality trees are pictorial representations of cause and effect logic that help lead to an understanding of the root cause of the effects observed or hoped to be observed in an organization. A Current Reality Tree (CRT) describes the organization as it is now, starting with observed Undesirable Effects (UDEs). The Future Reality Tree (FRT) describes organizations as we wish them to be, where the undesired effects are converted to Desired Effects (DEs).

Relevant, Achievable, Manageable (RAM)

The RAM tool is an instant assessment of how a project or effort can be achieved and what the outcome is likely to be.

RACI

The RACI diagram splits project tasks down to four participatory responsibility types that are then assigned to different roles in the project. These responsibilities types make up the acronym RACI: Responsible (those who do work to achieve the task; multiple resources can be responsible), Accountable (the resource ultimately accountable for the completion of the task), Consulted (those whose opinions are sought through two-way communication), Informed (those who are kept up-to-date on progress; one-way communication). It is generally recommended that each role in the project for each task receive at most one of the participatory role types. Although some companies and organizations do allow, for example, double-participatory types, this generally implies that the roles have not yet been truly resolved. This impedes the value of the RACI approach in clarifying each role on a task-by-task basis.

Storytelling

Storytelling is the often-ignored ancient art of conveying events in words, images, and sounds. Stories have probably been shared in every culture and in every land as a means of entertainment, education, preservation of culture, and instillation of knowledge and values. Crucial elements of storytelling include plot and characters, as well as the narrative point of view. Stories are frequently used to teach, explain, and entertain. Storytelling in business is a vital ingredient. If our customers and partners understand our story, it can be a strong positive determinant.

Stage Gate

This is the process of filtering or screening new product developments, at the appropriate time and before they consume significant resources. Robert Cooper, the creator of the Stage Gate process describes it as the systematic moving of a new product through various stages, from the screening process to product launch.

The screening stage is one that permits new product opportunities to be rejected early in the stage gate process. The stage is where the work is done, and the gate is where a decision to proceed to the next stage is given. One key issue at the gate should be to assess how balanced the project is between the intellectual, organizational, and human factors.

SWOT

A SWOT analysis is a strategic planning tool used to evaluate the strengths, weaknesses, opportunities, and threats involved in a project or business venture. It involves specifying the objective of the business venture or project and identifying the internal and external factors that are favorable and unfavorable to achieving that objective. The technique is credited to Albert Humphrey, who led a research project at Stanford University in the 1960s and 1970s using data from the Fortune 500 companies.

TRIZ

TRIZ is a methodology, tool set, knowledge base, and model-based technology for generating innovative ideas and solutions for problem solving. TRIZ provides tools and methods for use in problem formulation, system analysis, failure analysis, and patterns of system evolution (through the "as is" current state and the "could be" desired future state). TRIZ, in contrast to techniques such as brainstorming (which is based on random idea generation), aims to create an algorithmic approach to the invention of new systems and the refinement of old systems. TRIZ is a Russian acronym accredited to Russian engineer, scientist, journalist and writer Genrich Altshuller in 1946. It has become a popular methodology in recent times in DFSS (Design for Six Sigma) projects.

Value Chain

The value chain, also known as value chain analysis, is a concept from business management that was first described and popularized by Michael Porter in his 1985 best-seller, Competitive Advantage: Creating and Sustaining Superior Performance.

It is important not to mix the concept of the value chain with the costs occurring throughout the activities. The value chain categorizes the generic value-adding activities of an organization. The primary activities include: inbound logistics, operations (production), outbound logistics, marketing and sales, and services (maintenance). The support activities include administrative infrastructure management, human resource management, research and development, and procurement. The costs and value drivers are identified for each value activity.

The value chain framework quickly made its way to the forefront of management thought as a powerful analysis tool for strategic planning. Its ultimate goal is to maximize value creation while minimizing costs. The value chain is a strategic tool that helps assess how the core competencies of a company match the needs and desires of the customer.

Visioning

This is where a team collectively agrees on the desired future state for an organization, project, or task. Tools such as brainstorming are usually used.

Voice of the Customer (VOC)

VOC is a term used in business to describe the process of capturing a customer's requirements. Specifically, VOC is a market research technique that produces a detailed set of customer wants and needs, organized into a hierarchical structure, and then prioritized in terms of relative importance and satisfaction with current alternatives. VOC studies typically consist of both qualitative and quantitative research steps. They are generally conducted at the start of any new product, process, or service design initiative in order to better understand the customer's wants and needs.

appendix b

bibliography

Beckwith, Harry, *Selling the Invisible, A Field Guide to Modern Marketing*, Warner Books, New York, 1997

Blanchard, Ken, and Sheldon Bowles, *Raving Fans, A Revolutionary Approach to Customer Service*, William Morrow, New York, 1993

Blanchard, Ken, *Leadership Smarts, Inspiration and Wisdom from the Heart of a Leader*, Honor Books, Colorado Springs, 2004

Charan, Ram, *What the CEO Wants You to Know*, Crown Business, New York, 2001

Charan, Ram, *Profitable Growth is Everyone's Business:10 Tools You Can Use Monday Morning*, Crown Business, New York, 2001

Citrin, James, and Richard Smith, *The 5 Patterns of Extraordinary Careers, The Guide for Achieving Success and Satisfaction*, Crown Business, New York, 2003

Cohen, Gene D., *The Creative Age, Awakening Human Potential in the Second Half of Life*, Harper Collins, New York, 2000

Connellan, Tom, *Inside the Magic Kingdom, Seven Keys to Disney's Success*, Bard Press, Austin, 1996

Covey, Stephen R., *The 7 Habits of Highly Effective People*, Franklin Covey, Salt Lake City, 1989

Covey, Stephen R., *The 8th Habit, From Effectiveness to Greatness*, Franklin Covey, Salt Lake City, 2004

Friedman, Thomas, *The World Is Flat, A Brief History of the Twenty-first Century*, Farrar, Strauss and Gurroux, New York, 2005

Godin, Seth, *Purple Cow*, Penguin, New York, 2003

Goldratt, Eliyahu, *The Goal*, North River Press, Great Barrington, 1984

Goldratt, Eliyahu, *Critical Chain*, North River Press, Great Barrington, 1997

Gupta, Praveen, *Six Sigma Balanced Scorecard*, McGraw Hill, New York, 2004

Harry, Mikel, and Richard Schroeder, *Six Sigma: The Breakthrough Management Strategy Revolutionizing the World's top Corporations,* Currency, 1999

Hutson, Harry, and Barbara Perry, *Putting Hope to Work,* Praeger, USA, 2006

Johansson, Frans, *The Medici Effect, What Elephants and Epidemics can Teach us about Innovation,* Harvard Business School Press, Boston, 2006

Kim, Chan W., and Renée Mauborgne, *Blue Ocean Strategy, How to Create Uncontested Market Space and make Competition Irrelevant,* Harvard Business School Press, Boston, 2005

Mackay, Harvey, *Swim with the Sharks Without Being Eaten Alive, How to Outsell, Outmanage, Outmotivate and Outnegotiate Your Competition,* Ballantine, New York, 1988

Maxwell, John C., *Running with the Giants, What the Old Testament Heroes want you to Know about Life and Leadership,* Warner Books, New York, 2002

McCarty, Tom, Lorraine Daniels, Michael Bremer, and Praveen Gupta, *The Six Sigma Black Belt Handbook,* McGraw Hill, New York, 2005

Montablo, Thomas, *Seven Lessons in Speechmaking from one of the Greatest Orators of All Time,* The Churchill Centre, 1969

McGraph, Rita, and Ian MacMillan, *Market Busters, 40 Strategic Moves that Drive Exceptional Business Growth,* Harvard Business School Press, Boston, 2005

Neiman, Bennett, *Slay the Dragons, Free the Genie,* Chrysalis, Woodstock, 2004

Nightingale, Earl, *Lead the Field,* Nightingale Conant, Devon, UK, 1986

Perkins, Dennis, *Leading at the Edge, Leadership Lessons from the Extraordinary Saga of Shackleton's Antarctic Expedition,* Amacom, New York, 2004

Pink, Daniel, *A Whole New Mind, Why Right Brainers will Rule the Future,* Riverhead Books, New York, 2005

Rosenfeld, Robert, *Making the Invisible Visible,* Xlibris, USA, 2006

Sanborn, Mark, *The Fred Factor, How Passion in your Work and Life can Turn the Ordinary into the Extraordinary,* Random House, New York, 2004

Sjodin, Terri, *New Sales Speak, The 9 Biggest Sales Presentation Mistakes and How to Avoid Them,* John Wiley, Hobokon, 2000

Smith, Dick, and Jerry Blakeslee, *Strategic Six Sigma, Best Practices from the Executive Suite,* John Wiley, Hobokon, 2002

Stacey, Ralph D., *Strategic Management and Organizational Dynamics,* Pitman, London, 1993

Toler, Stan, *Minute Motivators for Leaders, Quick Inspiration for the Time of Your Life,* River Oak, Colorado Springs, 2002

Warren, Rick, *The Purpose Driven Life, What on Earth am I Here For,* Zondervan, Grand Rapids, 2002

coming soon

robert carter's new book,
SIGMAVATION, BEYOND BLUESKY

Sigmavation, Beyond BlueSky is Robert Carter's parable about BlueSky Aerospace, a fictitious company facing challenges typical in the twenty-first century. These challenges will be pertinent to all organizations, whatever the nature of their business. BlueSky embarks on a journey of enabling Innovation and business growth with the help of their brand of Six Sigma, called Sigmavation. Having secured sponsorship from the head of business development, the self-proclaimed BlueSky Sigmavators (Black Belts working on Innovation for growth) look across the company to seek out areas where Six Sigma has been used to help enable both Innovation and growth. Once successful projects have been found, the Sigmavators look for themes and patterns and then develop a campaign to create pull for Six Sigma for Growth from the leadership across the company. The momentum builds, and the demand for the Sigmavators takes off.

Sigmavation, Beyond BlueSky provides practical examples of how to move a company to out-of-this-world levels and achieve the success their efforts deserve.

Printed in the United Kingdom
by Lightning Source UK Ltd.
129572UK00001B/266/A